You Don't Know What you Believe...

until it's time to believe it!

Pastor Eric H. Jones, Jr.

ISBN #: 978-1-63752-981-2

Written by:
Pastor Eric H. Jones, Jr.

Library of Congress Cataloging
in-Publication Data

First Printing 2022
Printed in the U.S.A.
Merritt Publishing Company

Genre Category:
Self-help, inspiration, spirituality, Christianity, personal
development, confidence building, young adult

Foreword

If the Church has ever needed a practical, but powerful Word to develop and cultivate her faith, it is now. The writer of Hebrews gives a clear definition for faith in Hebrews 11:1: *Now faith is the substance of things hoped for, the evidence of things not seen.* The word substance means a foundation, or something put under, and the word "evidence" means a conviction or belief. Therefore, faith is the foundation upon which hope rests and the belief in a reality that is not seen. While this definition of faith is encouraging personally, many believers do not know this kind of faith practically.

This is the reality that Dr. Eric Jones Jr. conveys in this insightful, inspirational, and instructional work. Immediately, your faith will be challenged as you are compelled to examine and measure the degree of your own faith; to consider if the declaration of your faith is married to the demonstration of your faith. Dr. Jones provokes the reader to analyze whether his or her faith is only strong statements of faith that have not be tried. He then informs with a since of warning that all statements of faith will be proven and tested. Therefore, Dr. Jones echoes throughout this book that believers really don't know what they believe until it is time to believe it, and that the faith of many believers is based on what they have heard rather than what they know. Dr. Jones refers to this as intellectual faith rather than an experiential faith. Hence, Dr. Jones shares this profound insight, not merely intellectually but experientially as he processes his personal pain and experienced an unfamiliar hurt that brought his faith under fire. Sometimes God uses our personal disappointments and difficulties, as well as our pains and perplexities, as instruments to fortify our faith. Dr. Jones courageously and transparently shows us the struggle between his flesh and his faith as he wrestles with three enormous events that nearly compromised his spiritual equilibrium.

First, he grapples with his pastoral assignment to the saints and parental affection for his youngest son that announces his sexual orientation. Secondly, he tussles with the unexpected passing of his second son Kaniel and the undertaking of preaching his eulogy; and thirdly, he battles with a daunting medical diagnosis that has potentially fatal consequences and his faith in God's healing power. It is this trilogy of disappointment, death, and disease that inspired Dr. Jones to write this personally painful and powerful book that is guaranteed to test our theology and expose the flaws as well as the fidelity of our faith.

Dr. Robert C. Stanley
Hopewell Missionary Baptist Church
Pompano Beach, Florida

Endorsements for this Book:

After reading this book, you will attest that it is worth adding to your study material. This book will assist us when life dictates that we push off from the safety net of King Uzziah to a point where God becomes the focus point in our lives. *"And there came a day."* Our hearts anxiously await the next book to challenge our minds to go deeper into the lives of those who yet believe despite what situations life may have presented.

Oscar Chestnut, Ph.D

Pastor Eric Jones is skilled at taking complex ideas and simplifying them into practicality. Many people of faith chose not to struggle with issues of theodicy. We often retreat into a fantasy and hope for the best. In **You Don't Know What You Believe Until it's Time to Believe it,** Pastor Jones teaches that our beliefs will be tested, not to embarrass us, but to empower us to grow and serve.

Wayne Lomax, Lead Pastor
The Fountain Church, Miami Gardens, FL

Pastor Jones offers us his journey through the struggle of patronizing what you advertise; a journey of trial, transparency and triumph. A faith that cannot be tested, cannot be trusted! What an encouraging read. You will be blessed and challenged by reading this book.

Larry Covington, Pastor
The Ebenezer Church, Burlington, NC

Pastor and teacher Eric H. Jones has penned a practical and understandable guide to living a purposeful life. Written with overwhelming compassion, heartfelt gratitude, and thoughtful candor, this book is dripping with encouragement, wisdom, and basic truths about love and faith which are the guideposts for our mortal, earthly journey. It is a testament of faith and a beautiful manifestation of God's promises and unconditional love.

Tammy Reed, Education/Administrator
Communications & Public Relations Professional

My journey with Pastor Eric Jones has made it a joy and honor to endorse his book on Faith. What he addresses in this book is the reflection of his Abrahamic-Noahic-Jobain kind of faith. His call to ministry, developing a powerful ministry, decoupling many men and women for leadership, and service were driven by faith. This kind of faith is met with many challenges. His transparencies are helpful to all on a journey of faith. I am indeed blessed to have been a part of that journey.

Bishop Billy Baskin, Senior Pastor
New Way Fellowship Baptist Church, Miami, Florida

This book is a quick, yet powerful read. Readers will easily connect to the testimony while being inspired and uplifted by the message. Through the experiences of Pastor Jones, we are reminded that Pastors are indeed humans just like their parishioners. As such, they must process their way through the same everyday struggles, trials, and tribulations like their members. In this powerful book, we are reminded that religious leaders must too have lived the experiences that produce Godly wisdom to validate their Biblical knowledge. Pastor Jones, we will continue to follow you as you follow Christ!

Valerie S. Wanza, Ph.D., Veteran Educational Leader
Consultant/University Professor

Pastor Jones offers readers powerful and riveting testimony of how faith survives when confronted head on with fear and adversity. This empowering book offers practical guidance for anyone who has ever struggled with faith to know that situations are temporary, but God's promise for a better day is just ahead.

Burnadette Norris-Weeks, Esq.
Women of Color Empowerment Institute, Inc., Founder

It is in the midst of our personal trials and tribulations that our true character is revealed. The character of Pastor Jones shines as he describes in this book, in very vivid terms, just how he was able to overcome some of his darkest hours. It has been my honor to watch him live and write this book. Although his faith no doubt wavered at times and the foundation of his belief was rocked, he still glorified God and proclaimed the gospel, in spite of all that he had to overcome. This book will bless every reader because there is something in it for all.

Rev. Dr. R. Joaquin Willis, President & CEO
Collective Empowerment Group, South Florida. Inc. (CEG)

This book blessed my spirit! As I read through each page, I saw areas in my life wherein I struggled with believing that God's promises pertained to me. The situations going on around me caused me to doubt God's love for me, but after the storm had passed, I realized that *"it was good for me to have been afflicted"*. This book is a blessing to ALL because it reminds us of just how good God is, in spite of what it looks like in the natural.

Mia Y. Merritt, Ed.D.
Merritt Consulting & Publishing

I Witnessed the Unfolding of this Story!

To my husband who, with an attitude of patience, has always encouraged me to grow and develop my faith amid my struggles. You have been an example of the advice that you have given. I thank you for loving me enough to not allow me to settle for anything less than strength out of my weaknesses. Thank you for being the joy of my life for fifty plus years. I have watched you struggle through some of the most trying times of life, and yet you endured with strength, dignity and perseverance. It is because I have witnessed you go through some painful and disappointing storms that I know everyone who reads this book will be blessed. I can testify that authoring this book was not taken from stories read or the testimony of others, but from your personal experiences. It was through the refining process that God led you to see how to trust Him to be your light as you walked through your darkest hour. Discovering deeper faith often involves altering that which we have settled down in. This book will challenge you to move from intellectual stories of what God has done for others to a testimonial faith of what God has done for you. Through reading this book, you will discover that *"You Don't Know What You Believe - Until It's Time To Believe It!"*

Love Always,

Bloneva Jones

Introduction

I wrote this book in the aftermath of some challenging and painful events in my life. It was during the most painful and weakened state of my ministry that this book was birthed. I am aware that many books have been written on the subjects of faith and belief. However, writing about them and experiencing them are two different things. In the story of Job, these words begin his test of belief and faith: *"and there came a day."* These five words signaled the beginning of a period when everything he claimed as a believer was to be proven. When this happens in life, it is a time where we must swim, tread water, or drown. That day for me began when my youngest son came to me with a disapproving revelation about his sexuality. This brought about a pain of disapproval and questions of my failure as a father. My belief in God was not so much shaken as the way I demonstrated my belief in God. A few years later, my middle son Kaneil passed away from a blood clot. My faith and belief went into a tailspin. I had the grief and pain of a son that was absent and the sadness and disappointment of a son that was present. Then there came the attack on my body, which was my health test. I was diagnosed with bladder cancer. Soon after that diagnosis, I contracted the potentially fatal Covid-19. My belief was being severely challenged in various areas. It was one thing after another. The trying of my faith was being severely tested and my purpose was struggling to regain focus.

It is in our darkest hours that our relationship with God and our thoughts are purified. The depth of our beliefs is weighed and revealed, exposing the true object of our faith. Where do we turn to fill the void inside? To whom do we turn to comfort our deepest heartaches and heal our most painful hurts? During some of the most challenging periods of my life, I have learned and am still learning to embrace God's presence truly and not just theologically. I don't know how well I will do during my next storm, but I do have a few testimonies to justify keeping the faith and not losing hope through the ones I just came out of. In the aftermath of the death of my middle child, Kaneil, I struggled with why the Lord took him. I had just spoken with him that day and by that same night, my child was gone.

As I turned to the Word of God, which I had preached and taught for over forty years, I began to experience the wisdom that is gained through experience. Out of my grief, disappointment, and hurt, my generalized faith and belief became intimately personal. My spirit was inconsolable as I struggled with how to handle the disapproval of my youngest son's confession, the death of my middle son, and the diagnosis of my health. As teachers and preachers, we must not teach graceless lessons nor preach graceless sermons. Our belief can be right, but how we carry out that belief when dealing with sinners can be misinterpreted. There is such a thing as doing the right thing the wrong way. I also realized that death is an equalizer; it is the common denominator of all redeemed and unredeemed and belief must encompass that fact. Ecclesiastes 9:2 reminds us that, *"The same providence confronts everyone, whether good or bad, religious or irreligious, profane or Godly."* It seems so unfair that the same fate comes to all. In this life, there are some common aches and pains that happen to everyone. The Bible is like basic training when you enter the armed service. In that training, you learn discipline and you workout daily to increase stamina and strength. You are familiarized with your weapons and your enemies. This training equips you as a soldier, both physically and mentally. You wear the clothes of a soldier, have the discipline of a soldier, know the soldier's code of conduct, have the weapons of a soldier, and know the enemy that you are up against. You have the training, knowledge, mindset, and equipment of a soldier. You have the credentials of a soldier, but you don't have a soldier's experience, nor do you have the soldier's testimony until you have used all of your weapons against the enemy. The Bible is the basic training of a believer. It is where you learn discipline. It is where your strengths and weaknesses are revealed. It is where you learn about the weapons of your warfare. And it is where you learn about the enemy you are up against. What we know about God intellectually is not a testimony. Only when we prove that what we know intellectually is demonstrated in battle will we have an experiential believer's testimony. An unproven statement of faith and belief is accepted at face value, but only verified in the heat of battle.

Table of Contents

A special THANK YOU to the proofreaders
of this book:

Derrick Jones
Gisla Bush, Esq.
Tammy Reed
Tammy Walden
Valerie Wanza, Ph.D
Vegina Hawkins

I appreciate you!

Chapter 1

Believing the Day after *"That"* Day

And the LORD said unto Satan, Hast thou considered my servant Job, that there is none like him in the earth, a perfect and an upright man, one that fears God, and hates evil? ~Job 1:8

The book of Job is a familiar story to many Christians. It is a book that causes many to wonder why God permits bad things to happen to good people. This book is a demonstration of the strong faith that a God-fearing man had for his Creator despite the calamities and heart-wrenching traumas that befell him. Job was at the height of all Hebrew glory, with wealth, health, pleasant family associations, honor, prestige - the greatest of all the men of the east." More admirable however, was the beauty of his inner being. A man perfect and upright – so much so that with holy pride, the Lord himself said: *"There is none like him in all the earth."* Clothed in earth's blessings and crowned with God's favor, Job had everything! ...until that dreadful day happened:

On the start of that dreadful day, Job's sons and daughters were feasting at the oldest brother's house when a messenger arrived at Job's home with this news: *"Your oxen were plowing with the donkeys feeding beside them, when the Sabeans raided us. They stole all the animals and killed all the farmhands. I am the only one who escaped to tell you."*

While he was still speaking, another messenger arrived with this news: "The fire of God has fallen from heaven and burned up your sheep and all the shepherds. I am the only one who escaped to tell you."

Yet, while he was still speaking, a third messenger arrived with this news: *"Three bands of Chaldean raiders have stolen your camels and killed your servants. I am the only one who escaped to tell you."*

And while that messenger was still speaking, another one arrived with this news: *"Your sons and daughters were feasting in their oldest brother's home when suddenly, a powerful wind swept in from the wilderness and hit the house on all sides. The house collapsed, and all your children are dead. I am the only one who escaped to tell you."* ~Job 1:13-19

The story of Job is one that is heartbreaking, heart-wrenching, but one that shows the deep devotion and faith that a creation had with his Creator. We all can be challenged in our faith when we come face to face with our personal statements of belief verses the time to confirm that belief. From time to time, doubt can creep in and be intimidating. Doubt itself is not sinful nor wrong because it can serve as a catalyst to new spiritual growth. I have concluded that, in the case of a Christian, doubt tends to be circumstantially temporary and not spiritually permanent. Circumstantial doubt encompasses all the "whys" of life. Why did my child die? Why did my marriage not work? Why can't I find a job? Why did my spouse betray me? Why can't I find someone to love me? These are the questions that we meet at the intersection of biblical faith. It comes from the pain of living in a fallen world. In my experience, I realized that I had swept some inevitable facts of life under the rug. Seeing certain things happen to others but refusing to deal with the reality that those same things could happen to me became the greatest test of my walk with Christ. Spiritual doubt began to emerge out of my intellectual knowledge that had foundation in an experiential testimony. The challenge to my intellectual doubt was the awakening of a level of immaturity in my faith that needed to be addressed.

Many believers think that confessing unbelief is a sin, but it isn't. God doesn't condemn His children when our essential beliefs, which are rooted in Jesus Christ are questioned. Both Job and David, in certain situations, repeatedly questioned God, but they were not condemned. God's grace is sufficient to handle all of our legitimate confessions of unbelief that only seek understanding. Unbelief usually emanates as a result of looking at things that are happening around us in the natural. Struggling with our belief in certain areas is not a demonstration of a lack of faith. It is sign that we simply have faith that needs to mature. If we never struggle with our beliefs, our faith will never grow.

In 2017, a devastating test was dropped into the laps of my wife and I to the extent that we felt as if God had abandoned us. However, the Lord used that difficult situation to mold us. I will never forget that moment while standing in the emergency room weeping and asking, *Lord how could you do this to us. We were not perfect, but we were faithful.* I did not get an answer from God. As time passed on, the Lord began to mature our faith in Him, each time reminding us of His love and His promises. Many believers have discovered that when it was time to really trust and believe, they did not; and if they did believe in some areas, there were many gaps in their faith. Many Christians struggle with doubts and circumstantial unbelief, which makes them feel guilty. It is to those believers that my words are directed.

In the walk of faith, there are gaps where our faith must serve as a bridge between our despair and our destiny. It must be the link between our desperation and our deliverance, and a network between our pain and God's promises. We need to have faith in those times when the light has left and there is darkness all around. The Bible is full of stories where gaps stood between the call of God and that which stood in the path of that calling. I don't think that there was a greater gap between one's calling and their destiny than that of Joseph. God gave this young man a dream when he was 17 years of age. The dream was the beginning of a set-up. One day he was a favorite son and the next day, he was a hated sibling. The day that Joseph's pain began was the day that placed him on the path to bring God glory. He was thrown in a pit by his jealous brothers and eventually sold into slavery. (Genesis 37:28)

When the Midianite merchants came by, his brothers pulled him up out of the cistern and sold him for twenty shekels of silver to the Ishmaelites, who took him to Egypt. However, the Lord was with Joseph and his purpose began to unfold. Joseph's life was filled with what seemed to be setbacks on the surface, but in spiritual reality, they were situations that tested him, matured him, and ultimately set him up to bring God glory. Joseph was betrayed, lied on, and lied to. It is believed that he spent 11 years in Potiphar's house and two years in prison. There was a 13-year gap from his dream until he was promoted to Pharaoh's palace at age 30. One can discover a lot about who they really are the day *after* the worst day in their life.

When I entered the ministry, my belief, my vision, my faith, and my life seemed to be harmonious. I was grounded in the Word of God, and for years, I stood for what was right based upon the teachings of the gospel. My faith and life were one. They were indeed aligned. However, things got severely complicated when it came to "The day *after* that day." Job 1:13 begins with these words, *"And there was a day..."* The many vicissitudes in life which reveal who we really are, are continuously shaped by turning points, defining moments, and other experiences, whether we label them good or bad, choose them consciously or subconsciously, whether they occur by happenstance, or if we are pushed towards them by subconscious needs. And yet at the same time, there's always an inner awareness, a consciousness that most people are able to acknowledge, no matter how dim that light may be. There is a kind of underlying, enduring "self" that doesn't really have a form. It is just an awareness of its own. It is the self within yourself. Job had everything one could desire, including the highest praise of heaven, for God said: "There is none like him in all the earth" (Job 1:8). Job's *"day after that day"* subjected his belief to challenges regarding his faith in God, his perspective about God, his possessions, his family, and his personal health. He was the respected, prominent, affluent, faithful, prosperous Job who now faced the unknown path of the impoverished Job. There was the belief of the healthy Job challenged by the trust of the unhealthy Job. There was the praise to God for a happy family which was now confronted with the inner challenge of how to praise God when his children are now gone. The story of Job is about his prosperous and happy life before, and his deteriorating and sorrowful life after.

In the story of your life, how did you respond during your last major test? Were you angry with God? Did you question God? Did you question your belief in who God is? Did your faith waver? ...or have you considered how you will respond when the next chapter of your life begins with these words, *"Then there came a day."* I have an "After that day..." testimony that compelled a turning point in my faith. I discovered that there was a self within myself that I did not know was there. There was some untested faith, trust, and belief that had not been proven. The pain and grief of losing my son Kaneil at age 37 awakened a sleeping, unresponsive, untested self within me. I suddenly found my belief sailing in unchartered waters with unfamiliar landscapes. The book of Job can teach a lot about the "other" self within us that awakens *"After that day."* It is like an X-FACTOR in our belief. A variable in our faith that can have major and often unpredictable consequences or influence in our life. Job lost everything during the time of his severe test. He lost his family, his material possessions, his health, and his finances; yet through it all, he *never* lost his faith in his relationship with the Lord. When the bottom fell out of Job's life, he still maintained his confidence in his Lord.

Satan brought Job's troubles upon him on the very day that his children began their course of feasting. The troubles came upon Job all at once. Suddenly and unexpectedly, Satan leveled calamities upon the unsuspecting Job in quick succession. In the story, an unexcelled picture of complete despair sorrow, pain, and heartache is seen. While one messenger of trouble was speaking, another followed. His dearest and most valuable possessions were his ten children. The heart-breaking, heart-wrenching, devastating news was brought to him that they were all killed. They were taken away when he had most need of them to comfort him resulting from other losses. There are times of trouble in life when only God can help. Everything was done to heighten and intensify the effect of Job's calamities. They occurred at a season of celebration. It was a feast-day, and Job's whole family was gathered together in his eldest son's home. Without a note of warning, a fearful storm brought in an overwhelming flood. Job's story is akin to the man in the Bible whose fields prospered him, giving him opportunities one day, but the next day was the day of his death (Luke 12). We must make wise decisions on the day of blessings while preparing our hearts and minds for whatsoever happens the "day after."

And he spake a parable unto them, saying, The ground of a certain rich man brought forth plentifully, and he thought within himself, saying, What shall I do, because I have no room where to bestow my fruits? And he said, I will pull down my barns, and build greater; and there will I bestow all my fruits and my goods. And I will say to my soul, Soul, thou hast much goods laid up for many years; take thine ease, eat, drink, and be merry. But God said unto him, Thou fool, this night thy soul shall be required of thee: then whose shall those things be, which thou hast provided? So is he that layeth up treasure for himself and is not rich toward God.   ~Luke 12:16-21

If we could see the "day after," we would be much wiser in our choices the day before. In this life, as in the life of Job, unexpected disasters may follow so close to one another that before the first messenger is able to tell of the situation, a second messenger will arrive with more evil news. It's the old adage, *"If it aint one thang, it's another."* As bad news followed bad news, the last was the most dreadful. It has often been noticed how troubles come in batches. In Job's case, we see and understand the reason, but with most situations that happen in our lives, we do not know the reason. One fearful power of opposition is behind the whole series. Consider these verses:

Man that is born of a woman is of few days, and full of trouble.
Job 14:1 (KJV)

As if a man did flee from a lion, and a bear met him; or went into the house, and leaned his hand on the wall, and a serpent bit him.
Amos 5:19 (KJV)

Although Satan is the ultimate cause of all the tragedies that come into the lives of God's people, he does not inflict any of them with his own hand. He keeps that hidden and finds channels to send delegates from all corners. One day we may have a beautiful home and the *day after*, we are homeless; one day we may have an abundance of resources and the *day after* we have nothing; one day we are safe and secure, but the *day after*, we are not. One day, all of our children are with us and the *day after*, they all are not. Who can dwell in security when trouble may come in so many directions on any given day? It is impossible for the strongest man to secure himself against it. None of us can do more than make reasonable preparations, which may all prove futile. However, all may trust the providence of Him who rules the wind and storm and the hearts of man, without whose permission a hair of our heads can be touched. Our faith and belief have to be strong enough so that we are able to stand *"the day after that day."*

As in the case of Job, the worst came last. It is terrible for a man to see his resources disappear before his very eyes in a matter of a few moments; ...but when all his children are suddenly taken away, never to be seen again, that could have been the breaking point. That can be the catalyst that causes someone to lose their mind. The more intense we are in obeying the Lord, the more intense are the trials that befall us. Job's trials became more intense with each report, yet he maintained his integrity and he NEVER spoke ill of his God. Moses also discovered that the further he got into his journey on the road of obedience the more severe his trials were.

And Moses said unto the Lord, Wherefore hast thou afflicted thy servant? and wherefore have I not found favor in thy sight, that thou layest the burden of all this people upon me? Have I conceived all this people? Have I begotten them, that thou

shouldest say unto me, Carry them in thy bosom, as a nursing father beareth the sucking child, unto the land which thou swarest unto their fathers? Whence should I have flesh to give unto all this people? For they weep unto me, saying, Give us flesh, that we may eat. I am not able to bear all this people alone, because it is too heavy for me. And if thou deal thus with me, kill me, I pray thee, out of hand, if I have found favor in thy sight; and let me not see my wretchedness.
Numbers 11:11-15 (KJV)

Each day that we live, we must prepare our faith through the Word of God. We must be ready for *"The day after that day"* when our belief is tested. The adversary appears in the life of a believer to accuse, but it is actually the means by which righteousness is emerged and purified. It is after the trials have separated the chaff from the wheat that Satan is silenced. The doubts are quieted, fear is abated, anxiety is arrested, and the accusing spirit is rebuked. Job did not give way to any unbelief, doubt, or distrust in his Maker. He did not charge God with acting unkindly towards him but felt as perfectly satisfied with the adversity which the hand of God had allowed. Job's amazing response showed that Satan was utterly wrong in predicting that he would curse God before he died. Devotion is possible without dollars received in return. People can be godly apart from material gain. Job's belief and worship at the moment of extreme loss and intense grief verified God's words about his Godly character.

Spiritual Lessons:

❖ Many believers think that confessing unbelief is an unforgivable sin, but it isn't. God doesn't condemn us when our essential belief, which is in Jesus Christ, is sealed and the unbelief is circumstantial.

❖ There was some untested faith, trust, and belief that had not been proven. The pain and grief of losing my son awakened a sleeping, unresponsive, untested self within me.

❖ If we could see the "day after," we would be much wiser in our choices the day before. In this life, as in the life of Job, unexpected disasters may follow so close to one another that before the first messenger is able to tell of the situation, a second messenger arrives with more evil news.

❖ It is after the trials have separated the chaff from the wheat that Satan is silenced. The doubts are quieted, fear is abated, anxiety is arrested, and the accusing spirit is rebuked.

❖ Each day that we live, we must prepare our faith through the Word of God. We must be ready for *"The day after that day"* when our belief is tested.

Chapter 2

Believe! ...Even when Life Doesn't Seem Fair

Beloved, think it not strange concerning the fiery trial which is to try you, as though some strange thing happened unto you.

1 Peter 4:12-19

O
ur existence in this world is a mixture of joy and sorrow, agreement and conflict, happiness and sadness, war and peace, life and death. Each has its own time and season, and as creatures in this world, we must learn to adapt to the changes that are built into the cycle of life. There is no permanent state of affairs that exist in this world. This can be a great source of frustration because we fear what change will bring. We often do not understand why we are not rewarded for our efforts right away. However, we see the wicked who do not know God, the proud, who do not regard Him, and the evil who refuse to walk in His ways. They seem to prosper and delight in their successes and achievements on this earth. Consider what is written in Psalm 73:1-14 about this matter:

Truly God is good to Israel, to those whose hearts are pure. But as for me, I almost lost my footing. My feet were slipping, and I was almost gone. For I envied the proud when I saw them prosper despite their wickedness. They seem to live such painless lives; their bodies are healthy and strong. They don't have troubles like other people; they're not plagued with problems like

everyone else. They wear pride like a jeweled necklace and clothe
themselves with cruelty. These fat cats have everything their
hearts could ever wish for! They scoff and speak only evil; in
their pride they seek to crush others. They boast against the very
heavens, and their words strut throughout the earth. And so the
people are dismayed and confused, drinking in all their words.
"What does God know?" they ask. "Does the Most High even
know what's happening?" Look at these wicked people enjoying
a life of ease while their riches multiply. Did I keep my heart pure
for nothing? Did I keep myself innocent for no reason? I get
nothing but trouble all day long; every morning brings me pain.

We can neither be possessive of what we have nor can we understand God's purpose in giving them and then taking them away. We can only humbly accept who we are in this world and believe and confess by faith that God's way is right. To expect unchanging circumstances in a changing world will surely end in disappointment. To bring ourselves to accept our divine purpose in life will enable us to appreciate the seasons of transformation. When we come to understand God's plan for the salvation of this world, we will see that He is wise, just, and good. While we have time, let us seize the favorable opportunity for every good purpose and work in our own season. The time to die is fast approaching. Although there will be labor and sorrow for all in this world, there are also seasons of joy and hope for the purposeful. This is the strength to press forward, knowing that we always have something meaningful to do.

The different seasons of life can be beautiful and yet they can also cast dark shadows, shadows that remind us of the inevitability of trouble and evil that stalks every life. Sometimes we have questions that we want to know answers to, so we desire to ask God, but don't know how. When we were younger, we asked our parents questions because of things we did not understand, not because we were challenging their authority. There are things that the Lord allows in our lives that we don't understand. Life can definitely be challenging. Uncertainty can bring on clouds of doubt and scattered thoughts of unbelief. The vicissitudes of life can cause questions about the mysteries of divine providence. Although the Bible warns believers that we will suffer at some point, it is more often than not, that we have knowledge that is devoid of experience, therefore, we have no personal conviction of what we say. In 1 Peter 4:12-14, we find these words in the King James version of the Bible: *Beloved, think it not strange concerning the fiery trial which is to try you, as though some strange thing happened unto you, but rejoice, inasmuch as ye are partakers of Christ's sufferings...*

The struggle that confronts us is how God permits the righteous to suffer while allowing the wicked to prosper in worldly ways. At times, right seems turned upside down, and it does not seem as if God is true to His Word. It appears that being careful to honor His values and walk in His ways makes no difference at all. God *seems* to forget His promises to bless those who walk close to Him and judge the ones who defy Him. When He does not *appear* to be "good" to one that trusts Him, it can generate many perplexing questions. What happens to God's faithful can appear to be the very opposite of His many assurances that are very plain about who He blesses and who He curses. The question may arise: *Does it really matter to live a Godly life?* Job struggled with this mystery and so did many others. When it was time for me to really stand, I found myself battling between what I had always stood for and what was happening to me. The wilderness is an example of the obstacles that stand between the believer, his or her purposeless Egypt, and his or her purposeful Canaan. Moses was ready to die because he lost sight of God's purpose while being distracted by complaining people. Elijah ran in fear from Jezebel when he failed to recall the miracles that God had performed in his life. Gedeon was concerned with being outnumbered on the battlefield. We too can lose sight of our purpose when we allow ourselves to be distracted and overwhelmed by external situations, circumstances, and people.

When you look around, it seems that those who are ungrateful, proud, and Godless are prospering; and it can cause the child of God to conclude that life isn't fair. I am 100% certain that you have either said that, thought that, or heard that before. We see injustice on a daily basis. We see it on the news, we see innocent people killed in drive-by shootings, while murderers go free. We see unarmed Black men shot and killed by law enforcement and the officers go free. We see a double standard of justice when the same crime receives different outcomes because of race. In certain neighborhoods, we see people that are faithful to God going through much suffering while those who seem to live hard, carefree, debaucherous lives, remain trouble-free. In television and also in the movies, we see those who live lifestyles centered around money, materialism, fashion, big houses, fancy cars, etc. And these individuals seemingly get all they want: are able to vacation when they want, buy what they want, and do whatever they want - all while living lives that fail to glorify the Lord. On top of that, it seems that believers often have a more difficult life. You can walk into any church and find a list of prayers filled with people who are going through various trials. Many are in need of jobs, there are those who are struggling in marriages, family issues, finances, have health challenges, struggling with depression or other things that come upon the lives of believers. Not only that, but Christians have the struggles of striving to live Godly lives in a world that bombards us with temptations, while those who do not follow the

Lord, seem not to struggle at all. It does not seem fair. I thought that God, if He is truly Sovereign, would be able to bless the righteous and give the wicked his just reward. However, all too often, that doesn't seem to be the case. Have you ever wondered about that? Have you ever thought about how, in looking at the world, there seems to be so much injustice and life just doesn't seem to be fair? You are not alone. In fact, many of the biblical writers experienced some of these same concerns and expressed them in the pages of scripture.

One of life's puzzling questions is, how do we stand firm on the Word of God, even when life doesn't seem fair? Psalm 73 was written by a Godly man named Asaph who was gifted in music. He was a cymbal player who created music that worshiped the Lord. He was also a seer and a prophet with the ability of foresight. He wrote several of the Psalms, but in Psalm 73, he revealed his struggle in trying to understand why the wicked prosper and the righteous seem to suffer. It is alright to get totally honest with God about how we are feeling as Asaph did. In Psalm 73, Asaph gets very real as he reveals his struggle with the things that he is seeing all around him that seem to be unfair. Perhaps you have been there. I certainly have. I find it helpful that I am able to go to God's Word and find real people who had similar struggles to learn about how God still cared for them. Psalm 73 shows us how to relate to some of the things we see or experience; and it helps us to discover why we have struggles in the first place. Asaph knew in his heart that God is good and that He is good to those who are pure in heart. As Christians, we were also taught that God is good and for the most part, we believe that. Intellectually, I also believe that to be true. However, what I believe intellectually hasn't all been experienced by me practically. In verse two of Psalm 73, it says something that many of us can say happens at one time or another, "...my feet had almost slipped; I had nearly lost *my foothold."* Essentially, what Asaph is saying, and what many of us have said is: *"God, I nearly bailed on you. I almost stopped following you."* What is so poignant about this Psalm is that Asaph was a Godly man, a leader, who was revealing this. Maybe you have experienced this or are experiencing something similar in your life right now. You may be wondering why is it that the wicked seem to prosper and Christians seem to always suffer. ...or "Why is it that everyone else around you keeps getting blessed, but it seems that God has overlooked you?" I want you to know that you are not alone in feeling as you do. As believers, we do not always have the personal experience to back up what we believe. Oftentimes, we proclaim those things as true that we have read, but in reality, we cannot really claim things that have not been tested and proven. Without a doubt, circumstances can occur in life that can cause believers to question God.

The same things that caused Asaph to stumble are the same things that cause the people of God to stumble. There is a cognitive dissonance between what we believe in our heads (that God is a good God) and what we see with our eyes all around us (unfairness and injustice.) The two don't seem to harmonize. There is a disconnect. They don't *seem* to match up. What we see can be a great hinderance to what we believe. Note what the Psalmist said, *"When I saw the prosperity of the wicked."* The root of our problem as believers is viewing life through the eyes of the flesh. Once we see things the way the world sees them, we give Satan an opportunity to get a foothold into our lives and we start believing his lies. When we are viewing life through the eyes of our old selves, we start viewing life from the perspective of Satan. It may appear at times that unbelievers have no struggles, but the fact of the matter is that EVERYONE has struggles. However, there should be a marked difference between how the world handles struggles and how the Christian handles struggles. If we, as believers, allow doubt to creep into our lives as the result of lost, tribulations or trying circumstances, we open ourselves up to the deceptions of Satan to believe the lies that he tells us.

When we are viewing life through the eyes of the world, we start believing the perspective that Satan is trying to feed us. As Christians, we will be tested on what we believe. The essence of your faith in God will be tested during your most trying time. The true test of your faith will reveal how much you really believe God. If you trust him, then the trying of your faith will work patience. The truth may be that those around you, particularly those in the world, do have a better financial situation than you. They may have better material possessions, greater health, and the appearance of respectability; but the lie is that they have no problems. When we believe Satan's lies, we play right into his hands. Instead of focusing on the promises of God, we begin to let our adverse situations cause us to focus on the lies. Doing this will lead to drawing extreme conclusions. When we do that, we make wrong assumptions about our own beliefs and how we are living out our faith. From personal experience, I can assure you that it isn't worth it.

As I strive daily to live a pure and holy life, I still encounter pain, heartache, and sometimes confusion. I often wonder why the righteous suffer while the wicked often live in seeming peace and prosperity? Why the undeserved sufferings in the world? I see the unrighteous living ungodly lives without restrictions and I often wonder how that can be. They have the *appearance* of money, success, and fame, but in the end, is it all worth it? In the book of Psalms 92:7, it says about the this very matter: *When the wicked spring forth as the grass and when all the workers of iniquity do flourish, it is that they shall be destroyed forever.* Most of us have been at one point or another to the place of doubts and questions stemming from some unpleasant, devastating, or disappointing situation that has come into our lives. The truth is that our views can be distorted by events that have occurred in the natural realm.

Our perspective can become distorted by loss, pain, disappointment, and ultimately by Satan. Even if it was completely true that the unredeemed have no problems, but we do, we are only seeing snapshots of the present situation, not a complete picture of the victory in the end. What is it that enables the Christian to stand firm on faith when it appears to be failing? Well, first we must learn how to see with our spiritual eyes as it relates to the things happening all around us. We must then enter into the sanctuary of God. When we enter into God's presence, we begin viewing life through the eyes of faith. As God led Asaph into His presence, Asaph began exercising the faith that he had been given. Even when we exercise the little faith that we are given and begin seeing life through the eyes of that faith, we also begin viewing life from the perspective of the Sovereign Lord. It is from this perspective, that the things of this world begin to be seen in the proper context. We will be able to view the pleasures of this world appropriately, in their proper estimation, as well as the pains of this world. While the things seen in the world from the natural perspective may have the appearance of unfairness and injustice, when viewed from the perspective of God, we can see them from an eternal perspective. It is then that we can begin to have a better understanding of things. When we are viewing life from the perspective of God, we understand the eternity of the wicked and the rewards of the righteous. Understanding and knowing the hope that we have been given of eternal life, will help us stand firm and continue to persevere in this journey called life. As Moses lived by viewing life through the eyes of faith, so can we. Let's review how Moses did it:

By faith Moses, when he had grown up, refused to be known as the son of Pharaoh's daughter. He chose to be mistreated along with the people of God rather than to enjoy the pleasures of sin for a short time. He regarded disgrace for the sake of Christ as of greater value than the treasures of Egypt, because he was looking ahead to his reward. By faith he left Egypt, not fearing the king's anger; he persevered because he saw him who is invisible.
~Hebrews 11:24-27

Seeing through the eyes of faith will help us to stand firm. When we view things from God's perspective, the things that happen in this world no longer affect us in the ways in which they normally would. The anger, disappointments, distresses and rage that we would probably feel are not magnified to the degree they once were. We will then be able to say as Paul said in Romans 8:18 that, *"I consider that our present sufferings are not worth comparing with the glory that will be revealed in us."*

People do not always have the personal experience to support their beliefs. When what they claim to believe demands proof, their responses do not always align with their beliefs. The Titanic was designed to be unsinkable, which led many to believe that it indeed could not sink. One article described the ship as one with watertight compartments and electronic watertight doors, concluding that the Titanic was essentially unsinkable. Another article described the construction of the ship as *fundamentally unsinkable*. A deckhand was reported as saying that *"God himself could not sink this ship!"* Whatever the origin of the belief, there was no doubt that people believed that the Titanic was unsinkable. One passenger was reported as saying, *"I took passage on the Titanic, for I thought it would be a safe steamship because I had heard that it could not sink."* Another passenger wrote home and said, *"We are changing ships and coming home in a new unsinkable boat."* People had absolute *untested* faith in the science and technology of this new ship. The sinking of the "unsinkable" Titanic shattered much confidence in science and made people skeptical about such fantastic claims. Many made statements about the Titanic based on untested reports, while the ship was at the dock but untested at sea. The faith of many is still at the dock of proclamation but never proven on the sea of confirmation.

There is a story in the book of Mark 9:14-24 of a father whose belief fell short at the time of testing. The father was grieved that his faith was not sufficient to help his afflicted son. At the thought of his lack of faith, he wept. Nothing can be more touching or relatable to me than this. This father, distressed at the condition of his son, having appealed to the disciples in vain, now coming to the Savior, and not having full confidence that he had enough belief to be helped, he wept. Note his confession: *"I believe; I have faith. I do put confidence in you, but my faith is not as strong as it should be"*.

When my son passed away, I found myself sailing in untested waters of my faith. As a Pastor for over forty years, I had comforted many through teaching and preaching. However, when I found myself away from the dock of intellectual statements of faith where I had encouraged others to trust God, and when I found myself standing on the edge of my personal fiery furnace, when I found myself locked in the lion's den of my stated belief, the knees of my faith were weakened, and I questioned myself as to whether I could continue to stand. What do you do when your belief hits a wall? How do you escape when the walls of sorrow and pain are closing in all around you? How can you trust when you do not know and walk when you cannot see? Where do you turn when the *knowledge* of truth fails to comfort and heal you? What counsel can help when you find yourself standing tip-toed with your back against the wall of "why me" questions? Although I knew that God allowed believers to be tested by trials, my pain blinded me to that knowledge. I have preached a litany of sermons from Romans 3-5, where it reads:

"We can rejoice, too, when we run into problems and trials, for we know that they help us develop endurance. And endurance develops strength of character, and character strengthens our confident hope of salvation. And this hope will not lead to disappointment. For we know how dearly God loves us, because he has given us the Holy Spirit to fill our hearts with his love"

That verse tells us that the end result of tribulation is hope. This is hope that is faithfully grounded in expectations that cannot be cut off by suffering because it is founded on the goodness and truth of God and His Word. The experience is intended to develop and not destroy and to assure believers that we have not believed in vain nor exercised trust in a God who does not deliver. The problem with suffering is that it can momentarily stunt even the most faithful Christians. Suffering has a way of reminding us of the things in life that really matter, forcing us to depend totally on God, and thus refining our obedience to His will.

Because God loves us, He will keep us from being exalted above measure. Spiritual burdens are manifested to cure self-exaltation. When my son Kaneil passed away, that was a major learning curve for me when it came to my spirituality and what I professed to believe and know about God. I had to learn that as the thorn in Paul's flesh was said to be a messenger of Satan sent for evil, it was really God's design and He overruled it for good. Note that the lesson was not learned immediately. In fact, Paul prayed three times for the thorn to be removed. Prayer is a salve for every sore, a remedy for every malady; and when we are afflicted with thorns in the flesh, we should give ourselves to prayer. If an answer is not given to the first prayer, nor to the second, we are to continue praying. Troubles are sent to teach us to pray and are continued to teach us to continue instant in prayer. Though God accepts the prayer of faith, He does not always give us what we ask for, as he sometimes grants in wrath, so He sometimes denies in love. When God does not take away our troubles and temptations, if He gives us enough grace, then we have no reason to complain. Grace signifies the good-will of God towards us, and that is enough to enlighten and enliven us, sufficient to strengthen and comfort in all afflictions and distresses. His strength is made perfect in our weakness. Thus, His grace is manifested and magnified. When we are weak in ourselves, then we are strong in the grace of our Lord Jesus Christ. We go to Christ, receive strength from Him, and enjoy the supplies of Divine strength and grace. The strength of our pride is weakened when God is revealed as our only hope. When we accept our weakness, it becomes the place of God's power.

A believer should always be humble and contrite enough to acknowledge their weakness before the Lord. When they do, the Lord pours His strength into the believer's heart, mind, and spirit. The Lord empowers the believer to overcome and conquer all infirmities and weaknesses. The cause of my weakness was of a very painful kind. It was a deep soul-wrenching grief that was unfamiliar to me. It was an attack so severe that I questioned the very foundation of my belief. My trust in prayer was tested and shaken and my faith was significantly challenged. Death of the flesh is so final until you don't know what answer to anticipate. There were no words to be said and no answer to be uttered that would ease my grief. The more my doubts about what I claimed to believe haunted me, the more painful and obvious were the deficiencies in my trust and faith. However, as I began to reflect on more than forty years of God's faithfulness, it became clear to me that the successes that were achieved by me were due, not to myself, but to Christ. My weakness had always been His strength, for only by His grace was I able to stand firmly in my past, and it will only be by His grace that I will be able to stand now.

The stories of saints in the Bible were left for our example and encouragement. What we have in those servants of God are testimonies of the events surrounding their walk with God, an account of their lives written as a result of their struggles, some suffering or grief that they each endured. Throughout our Christian walks, God is developing in us, a testimony of faithfulness to Him and His Word under all circumstances. Our pain and struggles may be overlooked by others, and our faith may be hidden from all eyes but His. We may have no understanding from friends in what we go through and no cheering words from fellow believers in the fight for the prize. We may even have times when we hear nothing from the Captain of our salvation, but we must be faithful unto death in our spirits, our trust, our obedience, and our love. We tremble at the thought of the inevitable encounter with suffering and death. However, God assures us that suffering trains us in this life to be effective disciples until death discharges us from our purpose here on earth. To God, it is proof that we have fought a good fight. We are in a crisis of faith where we must decide what we actually believe. In this crisis, our faith is being challenged. The Bible tells us that David was a faithful servant of the Lord's: …and when his faith was challenged, he refused to rely on human wisdom for guidance. He asked for God's direction. Was this a crisis of belief since God said He would give David victory over the Philistines? Yes! David still had to decide what he believed about God. He had to trust God to do what He said He would do. The key to being faithful in a crisis is believing that God is faithful to His Word. When we first begin our spiritual journey, we often make decisions out of convenience.

Often, we decide what the outcome is that we want and then make decisions based on the desired outcome. If it is a positive outcome, then we will make an obedient decision. This is called outcome-based obedience. However, God desires that each of us live an obedience-based life. In order to transition from an outcome-based process to an obedience-based process, He will allow a crisis to come into our lives. This crisis is designed to create pain or discontent, which motivates us to seek Him to alleviate the pain. There is a place of painful obedience for everyone! However, this is not where God desires us to remain. Ultimately, God desires us to live a life of obedience and intimacy rooted in conviction. We obey His commands from a heart of love and devotion. During the crisis phase, we discover the personal love of God in our lives, which we had never experienced before. Most of us will get to this phase of our walk with God by first living a life of convenience, then we will go through the crisis that will then lead us into an intimate love relationship with God. The Christian life can be summed up in one word - LOVE. God's desire for each of us is to know Him intimately and to love Him with all of our hearts even in our crisis. To know Him is to love Him; to love Him is to serve Him; To serve Him is to obey Him.

Spiritual Lessons:

- ❖ Although the Bible warns believers that we will suffer at some point, it is more often than not, that we have knowledge that is devoid of experience, therefore, we have no personal conviction of what we say.

- ❖ People do not always have the personal experience to support their beliefs. When what they claim they believe demands proof, their responses do not always align with their beliefs.

❖ When we are viewing life through the eyes of the world, we start believing the perspective that Satan is trying to feed us. As Christians, we will be tested on what we believe.

❖ What lies between our faith and our destiny is a wilderness experience that exposes our imperfections.

❖ Prayer is a salve for every sore, a remedy for every malady; and when we are afflicted with thorns in the flesh, we should give ourselves to prayer.

Chapter 3
I Believe ... Help my Unbelief!

Jesus saith unto him, Thomas, because thou hast seen me, thou hast believed: blessed are they that have not seen, and yet have believed.
~John 20:29

The greatest roadblock to believers being able to fully benefit from their faith is not what we believe about God, but what we "don't" believe about Him. Have you ever asked yourself, *"What is it that I either don't believe or have doubts about, concerning God?"* The answer to that question is on the other side of the "but". I am inclined to believe that many of us can say, "I believe *in* God but..." The belief that's demonstrated in time of dependence exposes, either the maturity or immaturity of your faith. Strong faith in God requires maturity. In the book of Job, God called Job "perfect". Job was not called perfect because he did everything right. Like all humans, he felt the emotions that come with being human. It was because of how Job carried himself, his character, his dignity and his faithfulness that God called him perfect. Job was not always up. Sometimes he was terribly down, but he didn't stay down. He got back up. He was not always right, sometimes he was wrong, but he didn't stay wrong. He got back right. Job had so matured spiritually that his whole life was regulated by the Lord's will. To reach spiritual maturity, one must put away childish traits and behave like an adult. Immaturity would have rendered Job incapable of weathering the storms ahead of him. The heroic heart demands maturity because the immature person can neither withstand severe trials nor achieve great things. Drawing closer to God is the best fortification against the tribulations of the future. Your words and behavior reveal whether your faith is strong, weak, or spiritually non-existent. While it is true that everyone has a measure of faith, the question is "In who or what does that faith rely?" The believer will, at times, discover that in certain circumstances, they are disconnected from their faith. Nothing can be more of an attack on your spiritual confidence than realizing that your faith is not as strong as it needs to be when you really need it. How do we address the defects in our faith when it fails in our darkest hour amid some affliction, some grief, or some fiery trial?

Job was faced with a situation that called for faith and sadly discovered that his faith revealed some unbelief. However, what he was really experiencing was a weak faith. This weak faith was not necessarily unbelief, but an immature faith. Only unbelievers possess a non-existent faith when it comes to trusting God. True believers have taken at least one step on the way to faith that matures when nurtured. The hindrances which block the path of many are simply that they do not have enough testimonies that prove that they can trust the object of their belief. For many believers, much of their walk is by sight and when a situation demands they walk by faith, they are overcome with a sense of helplessness. What is needed in order to bring their faith into harmony and fellowship with God, is recognizing that they can do nothing to deliver themselves without the Lord. It is then that they will find the assurance of Jesus Christ who stands at the door of their hearts and speaks to their conscience, saying: *"If you can only believe, all things are possible if you only believe."*

The awareness of weak belief is an opportunity to feed your faith and starve your doubts. This opportunity only appears when there's a need to trust and you fail. Faith may and often does co-exist with a lack of trust and doubt. However, the discovery of unbelief should never make you doubt the reality or genuineness of even a little faith. There is nothing more troubling for a faithful Christian than discovering areas of questionable statements of belief. I realized during my time of testing that I had reached a natural breaking point which challenged several areas of my proclamations of faith. The dictionary defines a breaking point as a situation in which physical, mental, or emotional strength gives way under pressure. In our natural strength, we can only take so much hurt in our hearts before we reach a breaking point. That's when we either give up and let go or realize that our natural breaking point is the place where God has been waiting to become our spiritual strength. It is incredible what God can accomplish in the very midst of our storms and on the other side of the breaking point. One of the definitions of patience is the ability to pass your breaking point without breaking. When I read that definition, I asked myself the question, *"How can I pass my breaking point and don't break?"* Each of us have had moments where we were tested beyond our natural strengths. This was not an easy place to be. You will be surprised as to the number of Christians whose beliefs fail them at their breaking points.

In my times of testing, I had to learn that there was a blessing tucked away in the corners and crevices of my pain and grief. When I use to work out, I discovered that there is a place called the personal maximum. It is at this point where one can either press forward past their pain or stop at what they think is their limit. However, the greatest benefit of working out is on the other side of that breaking point. If you continue, you will discover that a major achievement is on the other side of that breaking point. In times of our weakest moment, God will come in and give you strength to know that even though it hurts, there is a blessing at the point of your pain. Brothers and sisters, you cannot give up now! The blessing is at the very pinnacle of your pain. God blesses us at our breaking points. When Elijah reached his breaking point, he went a day's journey into the wilderness in despair, sat down under a tree and prayed that he might die. *"I have had enough, Lord,"* he said. *"Take my life; I am no better than my ancestors"* (1 Kings 19:4). When we live our lives serving God and doing His will, we often know about trials, but do not prepare for trials. As Christian Bible-readers, we have heard about Job, Moses, Elijah, and Jeremiah reaching their breaking points and how in the end, their faith and belief in God prevailed. We rejoice in telling the end of their stories without considering they had to walk. Paths of doubt, disappointment, frustration and diminishing hope that had to be overcome before they arrived at victory. Moses was so frustrated that he could not meet the people's demands, that he said, *"Kill me now."* Consider the passages:

If this is how you are going to treat me, put me to death right now. If I have found favor in your eyes and do not let me face my own ruin.

Numbers 11:15

Job said, "I just can't take it anymore. I have no hope, I give up." What is my strength, that I should hope? and what is mine end, that I should prolong my life.

Job 6:11

Jeremiah was preaching God's word. As a result, he was beaten and placed in stocks. He said, *"I wish I had never been born; because he did not kill me at birth. Oh, that I had died in my mother's womb, that I ever have been born? My entire life has been filled with trouble, sorrow, and shame (Jeremiah 20:17-18).*

Be not afraid, only believe. We live in an age of suffering, uneasiness, panic and distresses. For various reasons, people are fearful, anxious, discouraged, and discontented. Doubts, worries, and times of despondency are common to mankind. Jeremiah often wept because of the sins of the people. He felt so low that he actually cursed the day of his birth. At one point, he vowed to never preach again. While in prison, John the Baptist questioned whether Jesus was the one promised. As a result of discouragement, Elijah went into isolation. Peter wept bitterly. Without a doubt, there are pressing difficulties that we face in this walk of life. This life is a scene of perpetual conflict. The many burdens that are encountered can cause one to become discouraged, depressed and despondent. However, discouragement is universal. Eventually everyone goes through it, both the saved and the unsaved, the rich and the poor, the strong and the weak. For certain, you have experienced discouragement at times, perhaps many times. You might even be discouraged at this very moment.

The days of our lives are marked by wounds and scars as a result of some pain, disappointment, rejection or grief while on this road of life. There are episodes of dark and dreary valleys resulting from the loss of loved ones, some failures or yielding to some form of temptation. For every child of God, there are seasons of plenty and seasons of drought. How you stand in those seasons will determine whether your faith is seasonal or eternal. Surely, all of us have seen great people that we admire, those who seem so strong. They appear to be boulders on the mountain of faith; then suddenly, they are blindsided by some unsuspecting turn of events. And then often, this happens while traveling down the path of over-confidence or a short trip down the road of self-praise. Then the question arises: "How could I have made it through so much and get caught off guard by such a seemingly small thing?"

When we take our eyes off of God, the Source of all that we have, we lose focus. It is during those times that the enemy sneaks in to catch you off guard. There are times in the battles of warfare you might get wounded by the enemy. Your enemy seeks opportunities to take advantage of the moment to catch you off guard and bring you down. All it takes is one moment of taking your eyes off God and focusing your attention upon something else. This does not happen because you are a hypocrite, but because you allowed yourself to get distracted by some struggle or careless moment. However, it's not the wound that will determine whether you stand until the end, but the character that emerges after the warfare is over. I believe that the church is being tested. God said in Hebrews 12:26-27 *"Once more I will shake not only the earth but also the heavens."* The words "once more" indicate the removing of what can be shaken, which are created things, so that what cannot be shaken may remain. Let us stand firm in our faith so that when the shaking is over, we will remain.

I've discovered that there are basically three means by which we believe.

1. Things that we read. These may include books, literature, newspapers, magazines, and certainly, the Bible.
2. Things that we hear from what people say. This group includes pastors/preachers, parents, teachers, news commentators, friends or family members.
3. Belief that's formed through experience.

Regardless of where your belief system derives, they are still subjective and objective viewpoints. Objective beliefs cannot be disproven, but a subjective belief is just that, subjective. Objective belief is completely unbiased. It's not influenced by personal feelings or opinions. It is verifiable through facts. Subjective belief has been formed in the mind of the believer. It often has a basis in reality but reflects the perspective of the believer's views of reality. It cannot be verified using concrete facts. Some years ago, I gave deep thought to the things that I believe about God. The question was not whether or not I believe *in* God, but whether or not I "believed God". This led me on a journey that exposed my unbelief. This was not a challenge to my belief in God, but what I believed about God. The dictionary states that to believe is "to accept as true; to have faith; to cling to; to accept the statement of someone as true." All of that seemed simple enough, until I found out that there are two ways to believe:

1. The first way is to believe that what is taught about God is true. This type of belief is predicated on knowledge rather than an expression of faith. In this case, the knowledge has not been experienced and there is no intention of experiencing the knowledge. I find this to be true in many statements of faith among believers.

2. The second way to believe in God includes trusting in and daring to be in relationship with Him. This means believing without any doubt that He really is who He says He is in His Word and believing that He will do what He says He will do. It means believing everything written about God in the scriptures.

Our belief is tested through the many difficulties and trials that surround us in our everyday walks. Some tests are purposely allowed by God to train and discipline us for higher developments of faith. If He calls you to a time of grief and sorrow, it may be to lead you to lift up the hands which hang down and the feeble knees of others. In so doing, drive you to trust more in Him, who has all destinies in His Hand. In the midst of gathering clouds and darkening horizons, the voice of God can be heard saying, *"If you would believe, you should see the glory of God."*

In Matthew 17:20, as Jesus gives a parable on faith, He says: *Because you have so little faith. I tell you the truth, if you have faith as small as a mustard seed, you can say to this mountain, "Move from here to there" and it will move. Nothing will be impossible for you.* Like the grain of mustard seed, being the least of seeds, it eventually becomes the greatest of all herbs, so must our weak faith grow. The little faith should be increasing, expanding, enlarging, growing, and strengthening from small beginnings, until you can perform the most difficult undertaking through faith. The principle of growth in the grain of seed was a demonstration of the potential that lies in just a little faith. Although the cry of a little faith is heard, like the potential in the mustard seed, the blossoming of that little faith holds the promise of a great faith. The beginner's faith which leads us to Christ, if not nurtured, declines. If the early zeal and success is not watered with the Word, your faith can diminish. As your faith declines, you may begin to doubt in times of testing. You may doubt the existence of your salvation and consider yourself a fool for your past conduct. Your path of life may become blurry while frustration grows as a result of faith without any effects. You may even deny the existence of ever having faith at all. Where will you run to or what will you do when your faith dissolves? When your faith seems to become powerless, you are likely experiencing an opportunity to grow. You have probably overlooked some vital points in the area of spiritual development. The chief error is moving from a humble state of mind. You fail to acknowledge God as your source of blessing. Once you begin to be blessed, you must not forget the source of your provisions! With each blessing, you must not get the crazy idea that you only without the help of your Creator, are the cause of the results - that you are the power! You may, as many do, begin to become spiritually big-headed. You may no longer ask that the Lord's will be done, but you will serve your own will. However, God is longsuffering and will continually encourage your growth in faith, even if you don't do everything correctly. If you're sincere, eager, and humble, God will be accessible to you and help you grow. However, if you become self-absorbed, you will slowly realize that your power has been turned off.

The Holy Spirit will not aid in your arrogant projects or self-destruction. Mercifully, God will patiently wait until you mature and return in humility and appreciation. When we are able to admit that our belief is being questioned, we can go to God for strength and clarity. With this acknowledgment, Christ can help our unbelief. How do you approach your belief when sorrow, pain and grief clouds your faith? I discovered that sadness can be very spirit and soul consuming. When I received the report that my son Kaneil had passed away, all the lights of my faith grew dim. I experienced pain like I had never experienced before. The pain was not physical, but a deep soul-wrenching spiritual heartbreak. The question that I faced was not whether God was faithful, but whether I believed what I proclaimed I believed. My struggle and tears revealed two things: my humanity and the weakness in my faith. Like the father in Mark 9 who brought his son to Jesus because his son had a dumb spirit, I too believed, but I needed help with my unbelief. My heart was distracted between my strong intellectual statements of faith and a weak demonstration of that same faith. I have sometimes, in looking back on the doubts and questionings of that time period, thought and perhaps even spoken of myself as unfaithful; but I was assured by God that I was not. My belief was as real as my doubt, and my mind was wavering between the two extremes: now a believer, and now a sceptic - the belief usually exhibiting itself as a strongly based foundation and the skepticism as the result of an untested intellectual knowledge. As I struggled with the helplessness of that moment in the days following, I battled to bring my faith into harmony and fellowship with God. I had to confess the immaturity of my faith and recognize that I could not do anything to change or help what had occurred. I had to stand on the assurance of what I had given to so many others, that Jesus stands at the door of our hearts and speaks to our needs and says: *"Come to me, all of you who are weary and carry heavy burdens, and I will give you rest."* I considered Job, who in the end, emerged from the crucible of trial with a faith that had been tested and proved. God's Word is the assurance that helps our trembling confidence to grow, and out of doubt gives us great calm in our darkest hour.

What lies between our faith and our destiny is a wilderness experience that exposes our imperfections. We often quote Paul's declaration after he understood the reason that God did not remove the thorn from his flesh when he said, *"When I am weak that's when I'm strong."* If Christ is truly our strength, then our weakness will manifest His presence and power. The key to this strength is the ability to stand when your outward condition and circumstances seem to be at their worst. It is the strength to continue walking during your darkest hour, even when you see no light in the distance. You must know that the light within shines brighter. The method that God used to keep Paul humble was to allow what he was going through to remain so as to teach him that divine exaltation must not lead to self-importance. There are times when we experience great troubles or temptations in the flesh that God often uses to suppress pride and increase humility.

Spiritual Lessons:

❖ In times of our weakest moment, God will come in and give you strength to know that even though it hurts, there is a blessing at the point of your pain.

❖ For many believers, much of their walk is by sight and when a situation demands they walk by faith, they are overcome with a sense of helplessness.

❖ In times of our weakest moment, God will come in and give you strength to know that even though it hurts, there is a blessing at the point of your pain.

❖ When your faith seems to become defective, you are likely experiencing an opportunity to grow.

❖ What lies between our faith and our destiny is a wilderness experience that exposes our imperfections.

Chapter 4

Believe That you are Being Developed, not Destroyed

My brethren, count it all joy when ye fall into divers temptations.
Knowing this, that the trying of your faith worketh patience.
~James 1:2-3

Very little can be learned about a person's belief during their times of comfort and ease. It is easy to follow God and have faith in Him when life is going relatively well. However, when we find ourselves in the midst of a great adversity, that is when our faith is truly tested, and we find out just how deep and mature our faith really is. As I look back at some of the events and situations that occurred in my life, I can see the times when my faith was tested the most - in the confession of my younger son being gay, in the death of my middle son and more recently, my diagnosis with bladder cancer. I confess that at times, sadness, grief, and fear almost consumed me. I am discovering with each new trial, that God wants us to follow Him whole-heartedly. Even though we may not know exactly why we are going through, what we are expected to learn, where we are going to end up or how we will overcome, God is still there. We have to hold on to the truth that is written in Hebrews 11:1 that, *faith is the assurance of things hoped for and the conviction of things not seen.* That verse is easily quoted, but it is no easy task to understand. After over forty years of pastoring, I still have moments when I struggle with my faith and belief. The trials are not always life-changing situations, but every day my faith as a believer is challenged. We may be tempted to give into our fears and think that we are incapable of making it through a difficult moment or situation but let me assure you that God does not give us more than we can bear, and He gives us the strength we need to make it through. When trials and tests come into the lives of believers, they do not come to stay, they come to pass. Nothing comes and stays forever. There are many situations in the Bible that start off with the words, *"And it came to pass…"* indicating that it was a test that was going to "pass" on.

When you have those moments when you feel you cannot make it, God gives you enough strength to make it through that day, then the next one, then the next one, until you are no longer in the situation or mindset where you thought you were not going to make it out of. We can trust when we cannot know and walk when we cannot see. Our finite minds can never fully comprehend the infinite mind of God or unravel all the mysteries which challenge our thinking. Jesus stands ready and waiting to calm our storms and restore peace into our hearts. God allows adversity in our lives to test the genuineness and reality of our faith. As cruel as it may "seem" He does allow calamities upon good men, not for punishment, but for purification and correction, just as loving parents chastise the children in whom they love. God's Word plainly tells us that we definitely will have tribulation. *In this world you will have trouble. But take heart! I have overcome the world* (John 16:33). Adversity improves the quality of our faith, so that we are able to say after the test, *"It was good for me that I was afflicted."* Adversity teaches us to be more thoughtful, more spiritually focused, more humble and prayerful, more grounded and complete, and more tender and sympathetic. Adversity promotes the permanence and growth of our faith. Adversity gives effectiveness, capacity of service, and usefulness to our Christian walk. Neither the good servant nor the good soldier are trained in luxury for his work. They have both to "endure hardness" and to pass through discipline if they are to attain proficiency and be of real use.

How do you respond when what you are going through struggles with what you claim to believe? Trials definitely put your faith to the test. All the testimonies and confessions which we have made must be proven. Those who stand in such trials give proof that their faith is sound. Because of the joy set before them, they are courageous, are patient while in the storm, and they are able to persevere. In difficult times, our belief can waver. Our hope can become dim, and doubts can cloud our faith. However, Hebrews 12:2 gives us the key to proving our faith in the darkest hour. Instead of looking at the situation and circumstances, we are to look to Jesus, the example of how to not only begin in faith, but how to finish in faith. His focus was on His purpose, which was greater than His predicament. Note that the passage says, "...for the joy that was set before him, He endured the cross, despising the shame, and is set down at the right hand of the throne of God." We are to look to His holy life, to His patience and perseverance in trials, to what He endured in order to obtain the crown, and to His final success and triumph. God gave Christ joy and strength that motivated Him to obediently endure the cross. He went through the trials, experienced sorrows in His soul, endured the torturing pains in His body, and suffered through the beatings, piercings of thorns, and tearing of His flesh with scourges and boring of His hands and feet with nails. And with all the evil that was inflicted upon Him, He was not weary of His burden, nor did He shrink or faint from it.

Before we can have the faith to go through our trials with joy, we must first have our marching orders from God which outlines our purpose. Although our purpose can be settled in our hearts, we might still cry out to God to *let this cup pass from me.* However, the Lord knows what's best and reminds us in 1 Peter 1:7 that *trials come so that our faith, which has greater worth than gold, which perishes even though refined by fire, may be prove genuine and may result in praise, glory and honor when Jesus Christ is revealed.* Just as the action of fire on gold separates from all alloy and unrelated mixtures and is proved to be gold by enduring the heat of the fire without losing anything of its nature, weight, color, or any other property, so genuine faith is proven by adversities. In this life, it is that gold is tested by fire, but man is tested by gold. The struggles in the life of a believer are like a refining process where what is not like Christ sinks to the bottom, and what is like Christ floats to the top. It is akin to being on trial to prove your faith. It's like quieting false friends that once were thought to be trustworthy but became witnesses for the prosecution. In like manner, it is like evidence that is used to challenge your testimony being thrown out of court. Although the misery, disappointment, frustration, doubt, fear, and pain can be devastating, it is important that you state your case with confidence. When we are being tested, God has us on a mission to put Satan in his place. It is in the midst of our struggles that we learn that wealth, health, family and friends are no foundation on which to stand. Only when the Lord is our advocate, priest and mediator, will we find that He will not only defend us, but in the end, bless us. Although the trial can take its toll and will challenge our character, the aftermath will reposition us for greater blessings. There are times during the trial when we might suffer terribly and question our faith. Resources can disappear, friends may add to your struggle, health issues can bring on depression and despondency causing faith and hope to be in doubt, loved ones can turn their backs on you.

When we look at the life of Job, he was a man known far and wide as Godly, upright and benevolent. Yet, suddenly he found himself in the depths of human problems, and his philosophical friends turned into prosecutors. They came to sympathize, but they stayed to criticize - and their accusations only added to Job's grief. Prosperity makes friends and adversity tests them. When the sun is shining and all of life is a joy, it is not possible to know true friends from false ones. When the storm clouds gather, most of them scatter like chickens in the rain, or we can say they "chickened out". The record of Job tells of only four who cared enough to stand by him. Only in adversity can one learn how priceless a loyal friend is.

These are just a few examples of what may happen to the believer during times of trouble and testing. However, the rewards of enduring your trial are sure worthy of all the trials that are endured. We deceive ourselves if we deny that there are some trials that we feel we cannot handle. I use the word "feel" because sometimes the trial or tribulation that has befallen us is so strong that it makes us feel that we will collapse under the weight of it all, but I find solace, strength, and assurance in knowing that God will not put more on us that we can bear. God encourages us through the following passage in Hebrews 4:15: *For we do not have a high priest who is unable to empathize with our weaknesses, but we have one who has been tempted in every way, just as we are yet he did not sin.* We also deceive ourselves if we say that we do not need divine assistance to deliver us when the storms of life are raging. Those who have learned to trust in God must expect their faith to be tried.

The Word of God plainly states that faith will be tried, and sometimes tried severely, but true faith expects trials and overcomes them, emerging victoriously. Trials are greatly for our good and greatly for God's glory. True faith, put on trial, will certainly bear every test, and that faith will be justified to the uttermost. We must trust Him also to the very end because outward influences prove nothing to us about God. We cannot read outward events correctly. They are written in the words that call for spiritual understanding. The Book of God is readable. It is written in human language, but the works of God are only understood by revelation. We are to understand spiritually that the trials of life reveal character and demonstrate the quality and value of our past training. We also need to learn that the child of God does more than talk faith, but they walk by faith, and not by sight. Our trust and faith are not in what's passing, but in the everlasting - that is not the seen, but the unseen. With his possessions gone, his children gone, his friends gone, Job yet says in 1:21: *"The Lord gave, and the Lord taketh away; blessed be the name of the Lord!"* That was faith that Job demonstrated, not sight. Let's look at three more demonstrative utterances of Job being rooted and grounded in faith and his fidelity to his God:

Though he slay me, yet will I trust him. (Job 13:15)

I know that my redeemer liveth. (Job 19:25)

...when he has tried me, I shall come forth as pure gold. (Job 23:10)

These scriptures were Job's anchors of faith and hope which firmly held his storm-tossed spirit. The value in the test of our faith is that it drives us back to foundational principles and rudimentary truths that are the basis of our belief. We are able to understand experientially the insignificance of the seen and the importance of the unseen. The loss of material treasures helps us to learn the value of an inheritance incorruptible and undefiled which does not fade. Faith in God's promises is necessary if you are to come safely through the pain and struggles of life. Job had a family, wealth, land and tons of sheep and oxen. He was doing right by God and suddenly things went wrong. He had no warning but was blindsided by it all. We too live in the land of Uz. Every one of us will suffer at some point. It is written in 1 Peter 1:7 that, *These trials are only to test your faith, to see whether or not it is strong and pure. It is being tested as fire tests gold and purifies it.* Your faith is far more precious to God than mere gold, so if your faith remains strong after being tried in the furnace of fiery trials, it will bring you much praise, glory and honor on the day of His return. You may be suffering right now and may be in deep pain. Turn to God and trust in Him and in His Word, knowing that He will bring you out. Trust Him who is a strength to the poor, a strength to the needy in his distress, a refuge from the storm and a shadow from the heat. Our God is a great big God. He is the Maker and Creator of heaven and earth. He made the sea and the dry land. He is the God of gods, the Lord of kings and a revealer of secrets. Nothing is too hard for Him. As can be observed in the life of Job, the aftermath of a storm that is allowed by God is not tragedy, but prosperity. As long as God is in it, all will be well.

Spiritual Lessons:

❖ When you feel you cannot make it, God gives you enough strength to make it through that day, then the next one, then the next one, until you are no longer in the situation that you thought you were not going to make it out of.

❖ Before we can have the faith to go through our trials with joy, we must first have our marching orders from God which outlines our purpose.

❖ Although the misery, disappointment, frustration, doubt, fear, and pain can be devastating, it is important that you state your case with confidence.

❖ You may be suffering right now and may be in deep pain. Turn to God and trust in Him and in His Word, knowing that He will bring you out. Trust Him who is a strength to the poor, a strength to the needy in his distress, a refuge from the storm and a shadow from the heat.

❖ The loss of material treasures helps us to learn the value of an inheritance incorruptible and undefiled which does not fade.

Chapter 5

Believe the Plan and Trust the Process

Then Job answered the Lord, and said, I know that thou canst do everything, and that no thought can be withholden from thee.

~Job 42:1-2

Belief is defined as "something that is accepted, held as an opinion, or considered to be true", although there might not be any evidence. It is belief that thinks a thing to be true than to be false. If the belief is unproven, the degree of confidence is below 100% because that which is believed is considered true but has not been proven personally to be so. As Christian believers, established faith in God and His Word should be more than just intellectual knowledge, but also experiential. If there is no personal evidence to support our belief, no test of our declaration of faith, we only have statements, but no testimony. If your belief is unproven, then it is insufficient justification for testifying that you can stand where you have never stood. Experiential proof helps us validate what we should and shouldn't believe. Even when we don't have solid proof for why we stand in faith, we still tend to boldly speak of being able to go where we have never gone and do what we have never done. Much of our belief has yet to be verified personally in the storms of life.

Who we are in our afflictions accurately reveals who we really are than what is seen in our comfortable circumstances.

I struggled with the reality of my youngest son telling me that he was gay. That confession caused me to revisit my belief pertaining to divine providence and God's abounding grace. I realized that there were some "tolerated" sins, but there was intolerance for other sins, in which my son was committing. The sin that he was committing was one of those considered by many not to be covered by grace. That confession of homosexuality to me by my youngest son brought about a pain in my heart equal to death. Then, the diagnosis of my health caused me to question my purpose and the professed vision on my life. Whatever my belief and faith was before these events, they were challenged afterwards. I had a before and after belief experience. Fear and doubt waged war against my belief. The battleground was my biasness in categorizing certain sins as worse than others. I realized that the things I preached against were biblically wrong and should be dealt with biblically. However, the correct manner of dealing with them under the covering of grace can be misunderstood.

My ears had heard of you, but now my eyes have seen you (Job 42:1-6). How real these words became in the testing of my intellectual faith. In Ecclesiastes 7:8 Solomon says, *"Better is the end of a thing than the beginning thereof,"* meaning that a conclusion of something is better than the beginning of it. What you say you believe has very little meaning until you can testify of how you responded and was delivered after being proven. This can be a testimony of the beginning of your trial - the struggle on the journey, the beginning of the restoration and the lessons learned. Because of the fall of man, everything is moving toward what was lost in order to become what it was originally created to be. In order for this to take place, creation is groaning. The redemption of man is the key to regaining paradise. For this to take place, three things must happen:

1. The process of trials and tribulations must expose our weaknesses and the sins that must be renounced and repented of.

2. Each bout of suffering must reveal the weakness in us that will be overcome as we allow God to become our strength.

3. You must only testify of what God has brought you through.

The stories of the Bible are testimonies of those who conquered their weaknesses. You can accept their testimonies of victories, but their testimony is not your testimony. Past victories are today's testimonies, and present trials that are overcome will be future testimonies. A personal testimony is not only intellectual knowledge but practical affirmation. A believer's testimony is the recounting of an experience of faith and victory that was practically proven in the heat of battle. This occurs when what is known intellectually has been proven by personal experience. Although we may accept by faith what the Word of God says, it is when we come face-to-face with conditions that challenge what we have read and what we have said that proves the strength or weakness. Our responses will testify for or against the faith that we claim we have. Second-hand information is no substitute for first-hand experience. In life, we are more persuaded by personal experiences which we have endured, than by the testimonies of others. It was only after Job's experience was over that he was able to say in Job 42, "...*I have heard of you. I have encountered you like I never had before. I have only heard of you by tradition, or from imperfect information. But now the eye of my mind clearly perceives you, and in seeing you, I see myself. My personal suffering allowed me to discover your glory and excellence and discover my doubts and questions."*

What is it that we learned from Job in the development of a testimony? He speaks his feelings; and although he falls, he is not utterly cast down. In the end, he comes to himself and to his right mind, repents, is sorry for what he has said, recants his words, and humbles himself before God. When Job needed support, his friends were in conflict with him, not only differing in their opinions with hard words, but were passing severe criticisms. The gist of their reasoning was that God blesses the righteous and punishes the wicked. Therefore, they concluded that Job's intense afflictions must be the result of the most grievous sins. When he insisted upon his innocence, they stated that he only added sin to sin by refusing to admit his wrongs. Job had been a man clothed in earth's blessings and crowned with God's favor. He had everything! He was in despair and wished he had never been born. He felt forsaken by the Lord, and in anguish of soul, he begged for death. He suffered bankruptcy, bereavement, body filled with boils, and a berating wife. It can trouble us today to see a righteous man of such character and faithfulness, so severely afflicted, so sick, so poor, so reproached, so slighted, to go through such tragedies. He was made the center of all the tragedies of human life. However, in the end, Job was healed of all his ailments, more honored and beloved than ever, enriched with an estate double to what he had before, and surrounded with all the comforts of life. After all that Job had gone through and overcome, he was enlightened and proclaims it in this scripture:

The knowledge which I had of thy Divine nature, and perfections and counsels, was hitherto dark and doubtful. That knowledge was grounded chiefly upon the instructions and reports of other men, but now that same knowledge is clear and certain. It is worth all the agony and misery of my bitter affliction. (Job 42:5)

When it seems as though all is lost and there is no sign of a breakthrough, suddenly the black clouds break open, and the glorious vision of God appears beyond them. Job now contrasts his new, direct vision of God with his former hearsay knowledge. A hearsay knowledge of God is what Job possessed in the beginning. Not that he was without any religious experience in those prosperous times, but the shallowness of it in comparison with what he has now attained makes it look of little worth. Most of us begin in this way. We learn of God "by the hearing of the ear only." This is especially true in a Christian country. Here, we seem to breathe a Christian atmosphere, and Christian ideas float in upon us unsought. But the faint perception of God that is acquired in this way cannot be of very great value to us. Historical facts can only be known by testimony, and the gospel must reach us through "the hearing of the ear." But we have gone a very little way when we have only come to understand and believe in the historical character of those facts. We are still only among the antiquarian relics at a museum. There is no life in such a knowledge, and it has little influence over us. We need a personal vision of God. *"Now mine eye seeth thee"* (Job 42:5). Job had longed for a revelation of God and he received one. But this was not in a vision like those of Jacob at Bethel or Moses at Horeb. It was the calm inward vision of spiritual experience which is indeed an experience of God. Seeing God for who He truly is, came about through Job's afflictions. In his great distresses, Job continually sought God. His grief strengthened his hold on the unseen God. Through his struggles, God spoke and manifested Himself. Faith is not a one-sided effort of man reaching after God, but through Christ, God's spirit descends to man, and the communion of God's Spirit with man's spirit is the deepest blessing in the faith experience. It is this type of interior vision of God that our souls need. We must go beyond the hearing of sermons to our own personal experience of God. Only then can we begin to understand Him. Only then does He become more real to us. Only then do we become more certain of God than our own existence. This awareness leads to humiliation. We no longer boast of our own rights or make the most of our own efforts and achievements, but we trust in God for all things.

Once the Lord manifests Himself to us, we experientially know that He truly is everything that we need. Our struggles will awaken our need for repentance and total dependence. In the light of God, we not only see our smallness, but we perceive our unworthiness. I discovered during my struggles and tests, that more was learned in the end than all the lectures and seminars could have ever taught me. My learning had falsely elevated me, and a certain amount of pride had begun to take root in me. However, the Divine wisdom of God, through my trials, revealed my mistaken interpretation of Him calling my son back to Himself. The Lord saw that I had been incorrect in questioning His will, so He allowed the enemy to test me. We never know ourselves until we see ourselves in the light of God.

Spiritual Lessons:

❖ A personal testimony is not only intellectual knowledge but practical affirmation. A believer's testimony is the recounting of an experience of faith that was practically proven in the heat of battle.

❖ In life, we are more persuaded by personal experiences which we have endured, than by the testimonies of others.

❖ Historical facts can only be known by testimony, and the gospel must reach us through "the hearing of the ear." But we have gone a very little way when we have only come to understand and believe in the historical character of those facts.

❖ We must go beyond the hearing of sermons to our own personal experience of God. Only then can we begin to understand Him.

Chapter 6
Believe the Word that you Have Heard!

They went right into the house where he was staying, and Jesus asked them, "Do you believe I can make you see?" "Yes, Lord," they told him, "we do." Then he touched their eyes and said, "Because of your faith, it will happen."

~Matthew 9:28-29

How much of what you hear do you believe? In Mathew 9:29, there were two blind men who came to Jesus for help. Jesus could have just touched them or better still, simply spoke the Word, and they could have been healed of their blindness, but instead, He asked them the question, *"Do you believe I can do this?"* Being blind, the two men could not see the miracle that Jesus was performing for them but had to trust what they were hearing. Much of what we need to believe God for is based on what we have heard. The Bible says that faith comes by hearing. When it says that faith cometh by hearing, it does not mean that all who hear actually believe. Faith does not exist unless one believes and obeys the message heard. We can preach the message and teach the message, but unless we respond in faith and unless there is evidence that proves that we believe the message, it serves no benefit. I came to realize in my time of grief and disappointment that there is a difference in knowing what the Word says and actually believing the Word.

Salvation saves, but it doesn't deliver from the things that constantly oppress us in this life. However, God knows how much we can bear and delivers us before we are overtaken. By the power of His Spirit, deliverance comes mentally, physically, emotionally, and spiritually according to faith and belief. When those blind men affirmed that they believed, Jesus was able to give them their sight. It is written in Mathew verse 29 that, "*Then he touched their eyes, saying, According to your faith let it be to you.*" I submit to you that we receive "according to our faith." Think about the way in which you think then think about the way in which you pray. The greatest battles of history have not been fought on the beaches of Normandy, the jungles of Vietnam, or the desert sands of Iraq, but the fiercest battles have been fought inside the human heart in the battle to believe. The devil is described in the Bible as the thief who comes to steal, kill, and destroy. He only has two opportunities to do that:

1. If God gives him permission for a specific purpose, as in the life of Job, or

2. If you give him permission through unbelief

The devil wants to steal your faith in the promises of God's Word, kill your effectiveness and productiveness for God, and destroy your life in every way possible. Think about the reason God permitted Satan to touch Job's life with pain and misery. It was to *prove him* to be the liar that he is. The devil knew Job by name and had already examined him fully and formed his conclusion about Job. The devil knows God's people individually. He knows our strengths and weaknesses. We are warned in I Peter 5:8 to "*Be sober, be vigilant because your adversary the devil, as a roaring lion walks about, seeking whom he may devour.*" He

works chiefly among the righteous because the wic
belong to him. The closer one is to God, the harder t
works on him. No one can be at peace with God wit
war with the devil. Job's initial response was to confess ...
miserable he was. One may say, that was a normal reaction, but
Job wallowed in his misery for a long time. For 37 chapters, he
wallowed. It was not until chapter 42 that he started making
positive confessions of faith. In Job 42:3, he said, *"I've been saying
stuff, when I didn't know what I was talking about."* I do not
believe that Job had to go through all the misery he went through.
He could have been delivered a whole lot earlier if he had done
what he finally did. AND WHAT WAS THAT? God wasn't trying
to make Job suffer, nor did it please God to see Job in pain. God's
only purpose was to prove the devil a liar and to reveal his servant
Job as a true servant of Him. Job's confession of faith set the time
that it took to bring his longsuffering to an end. When we look at
the patterns and character of God, we see that He does not change.
Because of their constant murmuring and complaining, the
Israelites delayed their journey to the land of Canaan, the promised
land, that land flowing with milk and honey. They complained so
much that God referred to them as "stiffnecked" people. In Exodus
12:40, it states that the sojourning of the Israelites was 430 years.
Like Job, the Israelites could have ended their struggle long before
they did.

There are times when we unknowingly give the devil
permission to bring misery into our lives through doubt and
statements of unbelief. God is omniscient. He knows everything,
including our deepest and most secret thoughts. The devil does not
have that ability to know all. He is supernatural, but he is not
omniscient as God is. The devil only knows what we tell him and
what is released out of our mouths. He loves to take the negative
words that we say and use those words against us, and he is a good

stener! We only have to say something one time, and he jumps on it with both feet. When we speak words of doubt and defeat, he takes those words, magnifies them, and if we do it enough, he will build a stronghold in our lives. He delights in manifesting the negative words that we say to disprove God's goodness. God has given us the authority to pull down strongholds if we have the faith to operate in our authority. The following words are written in I Corinthians 10:3-5: *"For though we walk in the flesh, we do not war after the flesh: For the weapons of our warfare are not carnal, but mighty through God to the pulling down of strong holds, casting down imaginations, and every high thing that exalteth itself against the knowledge of God, and bringing into captivity every thought to the obedience of Christ."*

The devil cannot read our thoughts, but our thoughts are the first step to our words and actions. When the Bible speaks of our heart, it is most often speaking of the place where thoughts originate. It is from that place that the mouth gets its inspiration, so God equips us to be able to correct negative and perverted thinking there, at its most basic level. Everything that is conceived in the heart does not have to be spoken out of the mouth. We don't have to give the devil permission to attack us, and if God gives the devil permission, we can be sure that He will be pleased when we resist the devil's temptations while using the Word of God with a believing heart. We have this promise in James 4:7 that if we resist the devil, he will flee from us. Jesus said to those men in Mathew 9:29, *"Let it be unto you according to your faith."* What you really believe is what you will confess out of your mouth. Are you confessing sickness or health? Regardless of how your body feels, what are you confessing out of your mouth? Regardless of what the doctor says, are you confessing life or death? Are you confessing poverty or wealth? Regardless of how much money you have, what are you confessing out of your mouth? The Word of

God tells us in Proverbs 4:23 to guard our hearts with all diligence, for out of it flows the issues of life. What you speak out of your mouth emanating from your heart, can change the very trajectory of your life for good or evil. This is why the Word tells us that death and life are in the power of the tongue and they that love it shall eat the fruit thereof (Proverbs 18:21). By your words, you shall be justified and by your words, you shall be condemned.

It is written in Hebrews 11:6 that, *"They that come to Him must believe that He is, and that He is a rewarder of them that diligently seek Him, for without faith, it is impossible to please Him."* What do you believe about believing? When you truly believe, it will drive you to action. Belief is not an unresponsive feeling. Believing is more than an intellectual acknowledgement that the Word of God is true. Believing is also more than having confidence that the Scriptures are divinely inspired. To truly believe means to have trust in the fact that God is faithful to His promises and to know that He is interested in every aspect of your life. The Bible tells us that God "is", not that God "was". Many in the Old Testament overcame tremendous obstacles and severe difficulties as their faith and belief were tested. They served a living God who helped them in amazing ways through His divine providence. Believing compels one to action.

We must diligently seek God by reading, praying, believing and simply obeying His Word while having faith that He will reward our diligence. The question may be asked, "Why is it important to *know* what you believe?" It is important to know what you believe because what you believe determines the decisions you make in life. Your beliefs will reveal your personal relationship with God by the way you solve problems. What you say will align to your belief when you speak. However, if your source of belief is faulty, the resources required in your time of need will not be available. Like the prophets of Baal, your calls for help will not be heard. Religious statements of faith are like clouds that carry no rain. Cloudy skies will not help flowers to grow neither will untried belief sustain you in a crisis. Although it matters that what you believe is true, it also matters the way in which you have come to know that it is true. In Isaiah 48:10, it is written, *"I have refined you, but not as silver is refined. Rather, I have refined you in the furnace of suffering."* Also, Zechariah 13:9 says, *"I will bring that group through the fire and make them pure. I will refine them like silver and purify them like gold. They will call on my name, and I will answer them. I will say, 'These are my people,' and they will say, The Lord is our God."* As believers, God is seeking our personal purification. In spiritual reality, all believers have been purified by the blood of Jesus Christ. However, practically there is still lots of work to be done. Paul writes these words in Philippians 2:12, *"Dear friends, you always followed my instructions when I was with you. And now that I am away, it is even more important. Work hard to show the results of your salvation, obeying God with deep reverence and fear."*

We are not to work "for" salvation but work "out" our salvation. Salvation is by grace through faith in Jesus Christ. But what we do with that salvation once we receive it is another matter. We are encouraged to develop the salvation that has been given to us as a free gift. We must believe that after we have believed and are saved, that within us there is the work of separating the pure from the impure. Life is filled with suffering, and the refining is intended to be therapeutic. God's purpose in our lives is not punitive, but beneficial. Our griefs and sorrows are designed to form the Diviner's fire in which God desires to separate us from our sins. What I have come to believe about my believing is that the refining is not designed to be looked upon as punishment from the Lord. Belief that is proven to be true after being tested can experientially claim a belief that is a bridge over the troubled waters of this life. This makes us not ashamed as we wait for the expectation of the promised hope.

Some of the trials that we go through in life are seemingly of a short duration while others seem to be long term. Since we cannot know the length of our trials, the best move while in it is to settle down and make the best of the situation until the storm passes. We must prepare to continue moving forward in life despite the trials that have come. We must take ownership of our situations without allowing those temporary setbacks to take ownership of us. That appeared to be the divine strategy of God for Israel during their captivity. Ownership requires an investment in order to benefit from the storm once it passes. While waiting for things to get better tomorrow, we must be productive today. Trials that are allowed by God have an appointed time and must run their course. Everything has its appointed time. Nothing comes to stay forever. All things come to "pass", and while we are in adverse situations, we must pray and look for the lesson designed for us to learn while we are in it. Even if we must sow in tears, we must not stop trusting and believing. The trials that are allowed by God are not merely punishment for sins, but part of the method by which He teaches us to fulfill the purpose ordained for our lives. Every divine affliction which comes upon the Christian is a type of captivity. Affliction is a state or period of being mentally or spiritually imprisoned, confined, or enslaved in some way.

When you find yourself in a position in which you would prefer not to be in, or when you are held back by the power of something over which you have no control, or kept from that which you desire to do, then look to the God that called you. These are the things in life that can be called captivity but should not drown your hope. Our hope is founded on the promises that every captivity in which the Christian is held hostage will have an end. Although we may be allowed for a season, to be discomfited in our present captivity, it will be for good and not evil in the end. It is a fact that no one can circumvent that in this life we will go through times of captivity. The Bible tells us in John 16:33 that *"In this world you will have trouble but take heart because I have overcome the world."* Regardless of race, creed, or color, there will be bright sunny days, and there will also be dark and dreary days. There will be periods of happiness and periods of sadness. The quality of your life depends on your faith in God and how you handle your dark days. The question is how do we go through and come out better and not worse? What do you do when you are going through it? The level of your trust in God will determine how you will come out of your captivity.

When you are going through times of trials, tribulations, hardships and difficulties, there is the temptation to put your life on hold. Waiting idly for the storm to pass is to allow opportunities to be lost. The opportunities to grow and become more mature is better achieved in your weakest hour. Life continues to happen during your trials. If you just stop and look around, you will notice that everyone and everything keeps moving. Watching the days go by and thinking of all the things you could do if it were not for the storm is pointless. Keep in mind that trouble does not last always. While you are going through a major trial, tribulation, or difficulty in your life, keep doing the things that you have control over, continue praying, and learn the lessons that are designed for you to learn, then prepare for the day when your trial or test will be over. Provide yourself with the necessities of life and mature in your struggle so that you may become a powerful person in the Lord when it is done. Don't abandon your faith, but continue to live in the fear of God, and He will give you strength you need to press forward and persevere in the midst of your temporary weakness. As a believer, your captivity is actually the work of God and can come in many forms.

God commanded Israel to settle down in exile and to carry out the normal functions of life while in Babylon. In other words, just because you are in a temporary state of captivity, be it mental, financial, emotional, spiritual or psychological, don't stop living a normal life. It may be hard to get up and function, but you must do it and you can do it. Keep pressing forward! Your captivity is not the end of your existence but the beginning of a new phase of relating to God. Do not rebel against your condition. Whether it be a situation, person, place, or thing, it is the authority of God that is over them for a prescribed period of time. In all conditions of life, we must not stop pursuing what we can have because we don't have what we want. Look for the best in your bad situation. Seek the good in it because there is always something good to be found even in the worse situation. When you find yourself held captive, then use that situation as an opportunity to grow.

Let godliness, longsuffering and patience rule your life while leaving it to God to work your deliverance in due time. There will be times when things look bleak. You may lose your job, your house, a loved one may pass away, or any of the vicissitudes that life may bring. No matter what happens in your life, there are ways to make the best of the situation. Time and time again, people make it through life's disasters with a renewed and refreshed spirit to grow and flourish. Problems can come into our lives causing extensive damage, but like many plant species rely on the effects of the fire for growth and reproduction, we too can adapt to life's circumstances and become more resilient and acclimated. Fires burn away undergrowth that hinders production but have beneficial effects. Every situation offers learning opportunities and an outlet to become better, stronger, and wiser in the long run. There are many examples of people making it through dark times and coming out spiritually stronger and more complete than they ever were before. The difference between those who crumble under the weight of the world and those who persevere is an enduring hope, faith, and resilience to make the most out of the worst of situations.

Sometimes we must pay a great price to reach a greater purpose. Enduring our captivities is the tuition we pay for a higher degree in life. Every real affliction which comes upon the Christian can be described as a captivity. To be in a condition which we never volunteered for can generate discouragement. To be held back by the power of something which we cannot control is the very thing in an experience which makes it a captive situation. However, every captivity where the Christian appears to be the victim will end in victory because *ALL THINGS work together for good to those who love God and are "the called" according to His purpose (Romans 8:28).* So if you love God, then whatever you go through will work out for your good in the end. For a season there may be discomforts in our present condition. However, we must not lose sight of the end, which God has in view in sending us into our captivity. He sees the outcome from the beginning. We may not see it, but God does. All the afflictions which He sends are like the hammer-strokes of the sculptor. Each one removes some imperfection or brings some new character into view.

Some people and situations are only agents the Lord uses to execute His purpose. It is possible to do better while you are going through than if you were not going through at all. God's Word to us today is to use our captivity to prepare for prosperity, not disparity. Build houses, settle down, plant gardens, marry and have sons and daughters. Allow your life to go on as normal. Instead of hoping for a quick end, seek peace and prosper while in your captivity. Pray during your time of captivity! In all conditions of lie, we must not abandon the comforts we can have today, because we think we won't have what we would like to have tomorrow. Wherever you are held captive, you must seek the good in it. Live in all godliness and honesty, patiently leaving it to God to work out your deliverance in due time. Remember, going through is not the end of your existence. As God's people, it is more often than not the beginning of a new phase of relating to God and experiencing Him on a deeper, more intimate way. ...so, don't rebel against your stormy because it is the authority of God over it for a prescribed time. While you are going through, seek the value of your refining fire because it will affect the situation in a favorable way. Most importantly, pray to God for the ability to turn your tragedy into triumph. You will be victorious in the end!

Spiritual Lessons:

❖ We can preach the message and teach the message, but unless we respond in faith and unless there is evidence that proves that we believe the message, it serves no benefit.

❖ We only have to say it one time, and he jumps on it with both feet. When we speak words of doubt and defeat, he takes our words, magnifies them, and if we do it enough, he will build a stronghold in our lives.

❖ We don't have to give the devil permission to attack us, and if God gives the devil permission, we can be sure that He will be pleased when we resist the devil's temptations while using the Word of God with a believing heart.

❖ We are not to work "for" salvation but work "out" our salvation. Salvation is by grace through faith in Jesus Christ.

❖ We must diligently seek God by reading, praying, believing and simply obeying His Word while having faith that He will reward our diligence.

Chapter 7

A Set up to Bring God Glory!

After you have suffered a little while, Christ will restore you and make you strong, firm and steadfast. ~1 Peter 5:10

There is no one in this life who does not stand in need of encouraging words, assuring promises, renewing trust, strengthening grace, enlightening hope, or consoling fellowship at some point in their lives. Discouragement is one of Satan's strongest weapons, because encouragement is one of mankind's most basic needs. All of creation needs and responds to encouragement. Even wives are a source of encouragement or discouragement to their husbands. As believers, we will suffer in this world. Not only do we bear the natural sufferings that all men suffer, but we are attacked because of our faith in Christ. However, the genuine believer has a great promise, and that is the assurance that God will take care of them through all the sufferings of this life. God will keep and preserve the believer and eventually take them home to glory. When we who are purposed by God watch and resist the devil, God will perform the rest. Our God who is the source of all grace, completes what in grace He began. He who called us unto glory will not let His purpose fall short of completion. If He chastises through much punishing, He sustains us much more in grace. Our confidence is in the assurance of the call, the glory to which we are called, and the way of suffering. The source of our calling is made possible by the grace of God in Christ.

I have come to believe that as Christians, we have been set up to bring glory to God. A set up is a pre-arrangement. It is prior preparation; it is putting something in position for a coming occasion. In creation, everything that happened after the fall was a set up. In Ephesians 1:11-12 (NIV), it is written: *"In him we were also chosen, having been predestined according to the plan of him who works out everything in conformity with the purpose of his will, in order that we, who were the first to hope in Christ, might be for the praise of his glory."* What Christ went through to bring about our redemption was a set up. Consider what is written in 1 Peter 1:18-20: *"For you know that it was not with perishable things such as silver or gold that you were redeemed from the empty way of life handed down to you from your forefathers, but with the precious blood of Christ, a lamb without blemish or defect. He was chosen before the creation of the world but was revealed in these last times for your sake."* Christ coming to redeem his people was a pre-arrangement that would bring God glory. What's happening in your life is PREARRANGED based upon the plan that God has for YOU. In Jeremiah 29:10-11, it states that *"You will be in Babylon for seventy years. But then I will come and do for you all the good things I have promised, and I will bring you home again. For I know the plans I have for you, says the Lord. They are plans for good and not for disaster, to give you a future and a hope."*

God will be glorified in the life of the faithful believer. Joseph was set up, but his suffering was the stage used to bring God glory. The story of Joseph mentioned in chapter one, was a set-up for greater prosperity that God had planned for him. Before God blesses anyone, He first must test them. Abraham was promised the blessing of a son given to him from both he and Sarah. God told him that the covenant would be through Isaac, and that through Isaac, Abraham's seed would be blessed. Yet, God told Abraham to sacrifice his son on the altar of mount Moriah, this very same son that God had promised Abraham that his seed would be blessed by. *"Take now thy son, thine only son Isaac whom thou lovest." (Genesis 22:2).* Abraham was obedient to the directive that God had instructed him to do, and when God saw that Abraham was obedient to the mandate, he blessed Abraham immensely, and provided a ram for the sacrifice. Abraham had to be tested first. He passed the test. David was anointed to be the next king of Israel, but prior to the promise being manifested, he endured many tests and trials. He had to run from Saul for his life, hide out in caves, and cry out to the Lord for help many times. There were no glimpses of him as a future king, but after he passed all of the tests that God had allowed him to endure and overcome, he was made King of Israel. All must be subjected to the test of obedience.

There are things that happen in the life of a believer under the watchful eye of God that are allowed and controlled by Him. Life is filled with what seems to be setbacks on the surface, but in fact they are situations that tests, matures, and ultimately sets us up to bring God glory. God uses trials that we go through to strengthen and teach us to endure and to mature in our faith. It might sound strange, but God permits evil, but from the evil, He causes good to emerge resulting in His glory. Good is designed to conquer evil. If not, God would be conquered and God would cease to be God. All the evil, suffering, temptations, and grief that we go through in this world as believers will end up working for good. One of the many quotes of Dr. Martin Luther King, Jr. was this; *"Faith is taking the first step even when you don't see the whole staircase."* I could not see the hand of God in the passing of my son. The clouds of grief and sadness was so great that my belief wrestled with questions and doubt, but grief must find expression. My son was a good man, a talented young man and a faithful child, yet God saw fit to call him home. I had to understand that I was only his guardian here on earth for a time, but it was God who was his Father. Faith does not promise an easy road for those who decide to follow Jesus Christ. However, faith does not disappoint. In the end, you will discover that the life of faith has strength in your weakest hour and gain in your pain. It is a universal law that strength is made perfect in weakness. A sense of weakness has a natural tendency to make us strong because it puts us on guard against temptation. We are never more in danger of falling into the snares of the devil than when we flatter ourselves that we are most secure. A sense of weakness is calculated to give us strength because it compels us to lean on our Savior. Self-dependence is a broken reed; it may serve us for a short while when there is no great tribulation to be endured, but when trials and afflictions come with their crushing weight, we must have the everlasting arms underneath us. The more we relinquish confidence in ourselves, the more abundant help we will receive from God. A sense of weakness has a natural tendency to make us strong by rendering glory to God and not ourselves.

In the weight of our trials, Christians become veterans in giving glory to the Lord. God gets the glory when out of weakness we are made strong. God gets the glory when we are enabled to perform activities beyond our natural strength or rise up from a state of grief and infirmity still trusting and believing. God gets the glory when, on the other side of our storm, we declare that *"I can do all things through Christ who strengthens me."* When I saw my son lying lifeless on the hospital bed, my words of faith were challenged. I was blind-sided by that sudden and unexpected circumstance and was caught totally off guard. My son, who was entrusted to me by God to raise, was suddenly taken away. Although I was aware that I was only his caretaker on this earth, charged to bring him up in the ways of the Lord, I did not consider that the Lord could return for him at any time. Our children are like the children of a king sent off to learn how to act in the palace. We don't know how long we have to do this, so it's wise to start early.

In my case, it proved to be providential because God came for him earlier than I anticipated.

Affirmations of faith are needed to give us mental hope in the face of life's uncertainties. Most, if not all religious doctrines are centered around some hope that is outside of the grasp of human attainment but necessary if one is to appreciate this present life. At that point in my life, my beliefs were called on the carpet. Not my belief in God as the Creator or Jesus Christ as my Savior, but my response to all that it means. I know scripture, but I have not experienced all that scripture promises. As a pastor, I have encouraged and assured many in the passing of their loved ones, but I had not personally experienced many of the things that I encouraged them in. I believed what I said to them because I believe the Word of God at face value, but without having experienced their storms personally, I was not sure how I would act in their actual situation. I did pretty good when my brother passed, a little better when my father passed, and even better with my mother's passing, but this was a new kind of pain. It was an unfamiliar pain, one that hit me in my soul. There were scriptures that I had quoted for years that now demanded proof that I had actually believed what I had quoted for so long. Some of those scriptures were as follows:

Philippians 4:11-13
I am not saying this because I am in need, for I have learned to be content whatever the circumstances. I know what it is to be in need and I know what it is to have plenty. I have learned the secret of being content in any and every situation, whether well fed or hungry, whether living in plenty or in want. I can do everything through him who gives me strength.

2 Corinthians 12:8-10
Three times I pleaded with the Lord to take it away from me, but he said to me, "My grace is sufficient for you, for my power is made perfect in weakness." Therefore, I will boast all the more gladly about my weaknesses, so that Christ's power may rest on me. That is why, for Christ's sake, I delight in weaknesses, in insults, in hardships, in persecutions, in difficulties. For when I am weak, then I am strong.

These are scriptures that I had quoted for years, but they were only effective when they became the light that shined through in my darkest hour. I understand, to some degree, why it took Job 42 chapters before he could say:

"I know that you can do all things; no plan of yours can be hindered. You asked, "Who is this that obscures my counsel without knowledge?" Surely, I spoke of things I did not understand, things too wonderful for me to know. You said, "Listen now, and I will speak. I will question you, and you shall answer me." My ears had heard of you but now my eyes have seen you. Therefore, I despise myself and repent in dust and ashes." Job 42:2-6 (NIV)

The things that have happened in my life will help me to become a better Christian and a more understanding Pastor. It will make me more aware of the need to show love to my family on every occasion, letting them know how much I care for them today just in case tomorrow doesn't come. The new creatures that we are in Christ must evolve from a seaworthy vessel of faith with untested Titanic statements to a proven vessel of hope. I must revisit some of my perceptions of the events of life that I held through Biblical knowledge without having Spiritual wisdom. Whether a situation appears good or bad, happy or sad, I must see them through the promise that, *"All things work together for the good of those who love God and are called according His purpose."* It was as though all that I had been preaching over the last 40 years was placed on an emergency room bed before me and I was asked, "What do you believe now?" Weakened and hurting, I later had a brief understanding of how God felt watching His son put on a cross and die. With it came a new appreciation of my salvation and the price that was paid. Surely, I will continually preach boldly the hope found in the Word of God. However, I must alert you that statements of faith, untested, is only belief waiting to be proven. We should all seek to live with the understanding that can be learned from the book of Habakkuk, who without understanding, questioned God's method when he asked, *"How can you do what you are about to do and still be holy?"* However, instead of drawing an immediate conclusion Habakkuk said: *I will stand at my watch and station myself on the ramparts. I will look to see what he will say to me, and what answer I am to give to this complaint." Habakkuk 2:1 (NIV).* Once he realized that God's plan always favored the righteous, his final conclusive statement was: *Though the fig tree does not bud and there are no grapes on the vines, though the olive crop fails and the fields produce no food, though there are no sheep in the pen and no cattle in the stalls, yet I will rejoice in the Lord. I will be joyful in God my Savior. The Sovereign Lord is my strength; he makes my feet like the feet of a deer, he enables me to go on the heights. Habakkuk 3:17-19 (NIV)*

Death is not the end for the righteous. If we are saved, then we have a destination, and this life is only a part of the journey to get there. You may be in the heat of a major test, just coming out of one, or getting ready to go into one. The events and circumstances of life are like a roller coaster with thrills and chills.

We have mountain-top experiences and we have very low valley experiences. We have good days and bad days, happy times and sad times, but the good thing about them all, is that God is always at the helm. He sees all, knows all and permits all. He even warns us of trials to come and tells us that, *"Your adversary the Devil, walks about as a roaring lion seeking whom he may devour"* However, He assures us by telling us that, *"You are more than conquerors."* He warns us by saying, *"In this world you will have tribulations"* but he assures us by saying, *"be of good cheer for I have overcome the world"*. Whenever we face a severe crisis in life, we need either a way to escape the crisis or the inner strength and knowledge to conquer the crisis. Many times though, we have no means of escape and no clue as to how to deal with the situation or predicament. It is then, more than ever, that we need the help of someone who has the power or resources to deliver us from the crisis. Just know, that no matter what crises we may face, there is wonderful news, and that news is, whatever you are going through, it is all working together for your good. However, there is a caveat …*"if"* you love God. If you don't love God, then that scripture is not for you and there is no guarantee that your situation is working out for your good. In the book of Romans 8:28, the Word says, *"And we know that in all things God works for the good of **those who love him**, who have been called according to his purpose."* You may not be able to see any good in your situation at the moment and it may not "feel" good, but it is working "for" good.

As a sergeant in the army, one of my jobs was to help keep the troops battle-ready. There were three stages that the troops had to go through before they were assigned to my squad:

1. They had to know themselves in a different light.
They actually got to know themselves in some of the most difficult situations. As believers, we must allow God to undo what we have

done to ourselves. We must also allow Him to expose what still resides in us that is not like Christ. Joining a church will not undo anything, that only begins a voluntary process; neither does it expose things that need to be removed from our lives. Isaiah was in church for a while before he got to know himself.

In the year that King Uzziah died, I saw the Lord seated on a throne, high and exalted, and the train of his robe filled the temple. Above him were seraphs, each with six wings: With two wings they covered their faces, with two they covered their feet, and with two they were flying. And they were calling to one another: "Holy, holy, holy is the Lord God Almighty. The whole earth is full of his glory." At the sound of their voices the doorposts and thresholds shook and the temple was filled with smoke. "Woe to me!" I cried. "I am ruined! For I am a man of unclean lips, and I live among a people of unclean lips, and my eyes have seen the King, the Lord Almighty." Then one of the seraphs flew to me with a live coal in his hand, which he had taken with tongs from the altar. With it, he touched my mouth and said, "See, this has touched your lips. Your guilt is taken away and your sin atoned for." Isaiah 6:1-7 (NIV)

One of the purposes of trials and testing is to help you see yourself as God sees you.

2. They must be issued the right gear and weapons.
Therefore, put on the full armor of God, so that when the day of evil comes, you may be able to stand your ground, and after you have done everything, to stand. Stand firm then, with the belt of truth buckled around your waist, with the breastplate of righteousness in place, and with your feet fitted with the readiness that comes from the gospel of peace.

In addition to all this, take up the shield of faith, with which you can extinguish all the flaming arrows of the evil one. Take the helmet of salvation and the sword of the Spirit, which is the word of God. And pray in the Spirit on all occasions with all kinds of prayers and requests. With this in mind, be alert and always keep on praying for all the saints.
Ephesians 6:13-18 (NIV)

We are told to put on Christ, put on the new man, put on kindness, meekness, humbleness of mind, longsuffering etc.

3. They need to know their enemy.
For our struggle is not against flesh and blood, but against the rulers, against the authorities, against the powers of this dark world and against the spiritual forces of evil in the heavenly realm.
Ephesians 6:12 (NIV)

In order to conquer an enemy, you must know his name, his habits and his place of abode. You must be familiar with who your enemies are. You must be mindful of the enemy you know, the enemy you cannot see, the enemy you can see, and the enemy you don't expect. Not only do we need to know our enemy, but we need to know who the enemy is using. Fundamentally, the devil is your eternal enemy. He is a sworn enemy of all the children of God. He pursued Adam and Eve from the beginning. He attacked the last Adam. He is busy looking around for you too! According to 1 Peter 5:8, he is "eager to devour" The devil also manipulates human agents to rise up against you. Consider the following verses:

If the Lord had not been on our side when men attacked us, where would we be?

Psalm 124:2

The arrogant are attacking me, O God; a band of ruthless men
seek my life, men without regard for you.

Psalm 86:14

The believer must be on guard at all times, alerted from all sides, prepared for any attacks, and always trusting God to be faithful. This Christian journey is a set up to bring glory to God. Joseph's betrayal, false accusation, and broken promises were set-ups to bring glory to God. Job's loss of family, resources, prestige, and health were set-ups to bring glory to God. I learned after much grief, sadness, and pain that Kaneil's death, although very heartbreaking, was a set up for me to bring glory to God. I had to realize that regardless of what God allows, He is still God and He is still worthy to be praised!

Spiritual Lessons:

❖ Life can be filled with what seems to be setbacks on the surface, but in fact they are situations that tests, matures, and ultimately sets us up to bring God glory.

❖ Faith does not promise an easy road for those who decide to follow Jesus Christ. However, faith does not disappoint.

❖ I must alert you that statements of faith, untested, is only belief waiting to be proven.

❖ In the weight of our trials, Christians become veterans in giving glory to the Lord. God gets the glory when out of weakness we are made strong.

Chapter 8

Belief That Believes God!

"Be of good cheer. For I believe God."

~Acts: 27:1-25

In order for weakness to become strength and for our struggles to bring God glory, it is not the light that we need, but the darkness; it is not the gentle shower, but a hurricane; it is not the prosperity, but the poverty; it is not health, but sickness. We need the storm, the whirlwind, and the earthquake in our lives. One writer said, *"If you want rain you must put up with the mud."* There are some things that you learn during the calm, but the best and most valuable lessons are learned during the storm. If your belief is worth its weight in salt, then it must endure in the severest storm and in your darkest hour. True belief will prove itself in the most severe storm. In my storm of pain and grief, I tried to control the attack on my faith and belief. I tried to make things better by quoting every scripture I had shared with others during their hours of grief. I tried to tighten the grip of my faith in an attempt to protect myself and preserve my peace. After many attempts, I finally learned that self-control can be a deceptive addiction and worry a constant companion as you realize that you really have no authority over the situation. Although I knew that Jesus Christ was the answer, in moments when it appeared that all was lost, my belief took a backseat to my hurt. In times of faith's greatest storms and deepest darkness, Hebrews 11:33-34 can put things in perspective: *"By faith these people overthrew kingdoms, ruled with justice, and received what God had promised them. They shut the mouths of lions, quenched the flames of fire, and escaped death by the edge of the sword. Their weakness was turned to strength. They became strong in battle and put whole armies to flight."* I have discovered that belief is not simply patience that passively suffers until the storm passes. Rather, it is a spirit that endures things with acknowledgement of the inevitable, and with hope. This is possible when we believe God. It is written in Isaiah 43:2 that *"When you pass through the waters, I will be with you; and when you pass through the rivers, they will not sweep over you. When you walk through the fire, you will not be burned; the flames will not set you ablaze."*

— In this strange world, the good and the evil alike must endure their share of storms. On board this ship of life we have a miniature world. A believer surrounded by unbelievers on the same ship going through the same storms on the way to meet the same Creator. How impartial are the storms of life? Paul and the crew set sail on a good day with the hope of reaching their destination safely. The weather report for your existence is sunny most times with thunderstorms likely sometimes during your lifetime. The gentle winds of life have a tendency of suddenly becoming a violent storm. However, God has sovereignty over circumstances. Christ can calm every storm, but He does not immunize Christians from problems that others in the world also face. Sometimes He miraculously delivers Christians from such situations, while at other times He gives us the courage to endure. We thank Him for performing miracles of deliverance, but also for His sufficient grace that provides endurance in the midst of storms. Life can paint a deceptive picture of calm that causes one to believe without considering the inevitable storm. Situations in life can appear to be favorable and the decision to do your own thing seems doable. A soft, calm, promising breeze may begin to blow, so we quickly loose anchor and set sail. ...but suddenly, things can change - in a moment, in the twinkling of an eye. Just when all seemed to be sunny and bright, the old enemy, the violent Euroclydon blows in. It comes unexpectedly, and suddenly you can't control your planned destiny. Everything in your life is abruptly uprooted, derailed, taken off course. Like a typhoon engulfs with swallowing power, you are driven off course making control of your life utterly impossible. Note the words in the book of Acts 27:15 when they said, *"We let her drive,"* that is, let the storm drive the ship at will. They could do nothing else. There can come times in life when desperate attempts to calm the storm will fail. Note that the crew attempted to save the ship with little success. The storm drove them under a small island called Clauda, and the island broke the wind so that they were able to take some measures to save the boat and their lives. However, the storm then drove them away from the shelter of the island, and all of their efforts to save the ship failed. Hopelessness and panic set in. They had been caught in the storm so long that all hope of their being saved had passed.

As Christians, we are called to be walking examples of belief and hope. Paul believed strongly in the sovereignty of God and was able to look beyond his bleak situations and anticipate the good that would come out of the storm. A vision of God's sovereignty may not come to us at once because our natural tendencies may be to panic, which clouds everything. When this happens, we must wrestle with God until we come out of that situation and are able to go to the people with a Word from God rather than with a public display of anxiety and distrust. The psalmist in Psalm 73:15, pondered the mysterious providence of God that can permit the wicked to prosper while the righteous suffer. After a sustained reflection on his doubts, he said, *"If I had said, 'I will speak thus,' I would have betrayed your children"*. As a result, without publicly proclaiming his doubts, he went to the sanctuary to battle it out with the Lord. There, he received a vision of God's sovereignty, and in the rest of the psalm he praised God. We too must wrestle until we see things the way God sees them. This will give us the confidence to be agents of hope in this hopeless world.

In the book of Genesis, chapter 50:15-21, After many decades after what they had done to him, Joseph says to his brothers, "*You intended to harm me, but God intended it for good.*" I have learned, and I am still learning, that you cannot give up on purpose because of what is in your way. The Buddhist calls it, "changing poison into medicine." Everybody has the inborn ability to create value out of any situation no matter how awful or tragic the situation may be. The principle of changing poison into medicine is that we can transform even the most horrific tragedy into the very thing that we need to become better than we are presently. This concept isn't just a Buddhism philosophy, but the ancient Stoics believed the same thing. Marcus Aurelius wrote the following: "*Our actions may be impeded, but there can be no impeding of our intentions or dispositions because we can accommodate and adapt.* The mind adapts to obstacles by turning adversity into advantage. The impediment which was intended to block purpose actually advances purpose. What stands in the way becomes the way. This notion that the obstacles that prevent us from achieving our purpose can be used and, in some cases, may even be necessary to achieve our purpose does not seem logical. One may wonder if an obstacle lies in the way, how then can it possibly be used to achieve one's purpose? There are different answers depending on the obstacle itself.

Sometimes failure itself is a benefit. There is failure that forces one to pursue an alternative path that otherwise would not have been considered. It is then discovered that the alternative way turns out to be the best way, if not sometimes the only way, to achieve purpose. At other times, the true obstacle is not the obstacle in front of us but the obstacle inside of us. Perhaps the obstacle is our inability to be flexible, our arrogance, pride, unwillingness to forgive others or our fears. However, when victory over external obstacles is determined by victory over internal ones, we are then trained by those obstacles. Joseph faced obstacle after obstacle, but in the end, God's purpose for his life was fulfilled. Although Joseph knew God, he was not able to comprehend in the slightest what God had planned for him. But in the end, the purpose of God unfolded in his life. Joseph's purpose came into fruition in a way that no one who knew him along the way would have ever imagined. Joseph declared that God had overruled their evil and worked it out for his good. He had seen God's hand in all the adverse circumstances of his life and how God worked them all out for his good. God had used all of Joseph's trials to strengthen him, build his character, and to teach him to endure, and work in a spirit of excellence. Considering all that Joseph had gone through from the betrayal of his own flesh and blood to being falsely and wrongly accused, to even being forgotten about after he revealed the dreams of the baker and butler while in prison, he could have given up on God. He could have said that if there was a God who truly cared for him, He would not have allowed such devastating circumstances to befall him, but in spite of all that Joseph went through, he still maintained his integrity and walked in the ways of righteousness. He refused to give up on God.

How many of us give up on God when bad things happen? …when we lose a loved one? …when we lose a house, car or other material possessions? …when someone we love gets incarcerated. …when a marriage falls apart. Things falling apart in the natural could actually be things coming together in the spirit. Notwithstanding all that happened, Joseph did not give up on his

God. He passed his tests and he was blessed afterwards. Thus, God was able to exalt him to be the ruler of Egypt so that he could save the world of his day from utter catastrophe from the famine. With us, as with Joseph, when encountering obstacles, benefits often arise that we never expect. Even when it appears that we are blocked from obtaining our purpose, God will open up opportunities that are even better than what we wanted originally and give us a victory even greater than we expected. Another benefit of going through the fiery furnace of trials is that we become uniquely positioned to offer support and hope to others going through the same thing that we went through. Encountering obstacles is considered inconsistent to the path of purpose, but only in facing a strong enemy are we able to become strong in our pursuit of purpose.

Only in developing strength can we navigate life's challenges with a sense of confidence and calm. Even if an obstacle appears to prevent you from attaining your purpose, as you faithfully trust God, patiently wait to overcome it, you will learn something that will serve you well throughout your Christian journey. The divine mode of conduct in the face of adversity is understanding that God permits evil, but from the evil, He constantly causes good to emerge. If good were not destined to conquer evil, God would be conquered, or rather God would cease to be. This law appears full of light when we read the history of such men as Joseph, Moses, and David. It is, however, nowhere more evident than in the life of Jesus Christ. Here, evil stands out in its most appalling intensity, and from that very excess comes forth the salvation of mankind. Since the scriptures call us to be imitators of Christ, like Him, we must endeavor to draw good out of evil. For believing souls there is a divine testing. Its aim is to transform evil into good. Evil, considered as a trial, comes from three different sources: from God, through the afflictions of life;

from men, through their animosity or from even ourselves, through our own faults. We may learn divine lessons from sorrow and grief, gain strength in our times of weakness, learn lessons of wisdom from our experiences, increase discernment from our enemies, and gather instructions from our faults. Just know that God is our refuge and strength, a very present help in time of troubles.

Spiritual Lessons:

- ❖ There is failure that forces one to pursue an alternative path that otherwise would not have been considered. It is then discovered that the alternative way turns out to be the best way, if not sometimes the only way, to achieve purpose.

- ❖ Even when it appears that we are blocked from obtaining our purpose, God will open up opportunities that are even better than what we wanted originally and give us a victory even greater than we expected.

- ❖ Only in developing strength can we navigate life's challenges with a sense of confidence and calm.

- ❖ If good were not destined to conquer evil, God would be conquered, or rather God would cease to be.

- ❖ Things falling apart in the natural could actually be things coming together in the spirit.

Chapter 9

The Mission of Suffering & Pain Proves Belief

Let us hold fast the profession of our faith without wavering; for he is faithful that promised. ~Hebrews 10:2

The legacy of suffering began with the curse. There was the creation, the curse, then the cure. The cure enables us to overcome the effects of the curse. Everything in nature must struggle and suffer to become, in purpose, what God intended. A man found a cocoon of the emperor moth and took it home to watch it emerge. One day a small opening appeared, and for several hours the moth struggled but could not seem to force its body past a certain point. Deciding something was wrong, the man took scissors and snipped the remaining bit of cocoon. The moth emerged easily, its body large and swollen, the wings small and shriveled. He expected that in a few hours the wings would spread out in their natural beauty, but they did not. Instead of developing into a creature free to fly, the moth spent its life dragging around a swollen body and shriveled wings. The constricting cocoon and the struggle necessary to pass through the tiny opening are God's way of forcing fluid from the body into the wings. The "merciful" snip was, in reality, cruel and obstructed what was to be a natural process necessary for growth, maturity and strength. Sometimes the struggle is exactly what we need. If we were to go through our life without any obstacles, we would be crippled. The chick must break the egg, the seed must die, the ground must be broken up. Suffering happens to the good, bad, the penitent and it happened to the Son of God. The thief on the cross was crucified, the penitent thief was crucified, and the Son of God was crucified. Each one died on the cross. These paint a picture of the fact that struggle and suffering often precedes blessing. When it comes to belief and suffering, Philippians 1:29 says: *"...For unto you it is given in the behalf of Christ, not only to believe on him, but also to suffer for his sake..."* Paul saw suffering as a privilege, a declaration which may sound strange to the world. However, suffering is frequently mentioned in the New Testament. It is said of the apostles in Acts 5:41 that, *"...they departed from the presence of the council, rejoicing that they were counted worthy to suffer shame for his name."* Furthermore, in Colossians 1:24 (NIV), it reads, *Now I rejoice in what was suffered for you, and I fill up in my flesh what is still lacking in regard to Christ's afflictions, for the sake of his body, which is the church.* Additionally, 1 Peter 4:13 states this concerning suffering: *"...But rejoice, inasmuch as ye are partakers of Christ's sufferings."*

In this life, we wrestle with the reality of the curse of evil, sin, and death. Tragedies and diseases affect our families, friends, and even our own lives. Suffering in the scriptures, much like our own suffering, isn't neat, tidy, or systematic. Life is often more complex than clear. While there is no way to answer all questions regarding suffering, it might be helpful to look at some kinds of suffering and affliction seen throughout the scriptures. In massive tragedies, multiple kinds of suffering are occurring at the same time affecting countless people in numerous ways. As believers we're not isolated from suffering. Everyone suffers at some point in life. We may suffer from situations emanating through or with family, friends, or personal health and grief. In the case of a believer, God chastens us in order to mature us. While this kind of suffering is not pleasant at the time, we later see the effects of God's work and thank Him for continually allowing suffering for our growth in holiness and fruitfulness. As believers, we are called to live lives that are spiritually grounded in God. As we live, move, and have our being, His power dwells in us. The power of God which guards the believer is no external force working upon us from without, but the spiritual power of God that works within, in which He lives, and with whose Spirit we are clothed. By the power of God in every tribulation, we are kept unto salvation as we walk by faith. It is through this faith that in those hours and days when the clouds return after the rain, that we are kept by the Power of God. In the book of Hebrews 11:1-39, we learn that suffering in life ranges from minor to severe. However, one thing is certain, everyone will face some hurt, some affliction, some troubling situation or find themselves distressed due to the pressure of circumstances or conflict with people. Pain can be termed as suffering's first cousin. Pain is one of the tools that God uses to discipline us.

In Job 33:19, it is written that, *"God disciplines people with pain on their sickbeds, with ceaseless aching in their bones."* God often afflicts the body for the good of the soul. Believing this will greatly enhance your ability to receive the intended conversion and blessing from your pain and suffering. Pain is the fruit of sin, but the grace of God is often made a means of good to the soul. When afflictions have done their work, they will be removed. God makes use of pain to awaken and convert his chosen. In the hand of God, suffering and pain, although uncomfortable, benefits the one who endures. In Psalm 119:67-75, David testifies as follows:

I used to wander off until you disciplined me; but now I closely follow your word. You are good and do only good; teach me your decrees. Arrogant people smear me with lies, but in truth I obey your commandments with all my heart. Their hearts are dull and stupid, but I delight in your instructions. My suffering was good for me, for it taught me to pay attention to your decrees. Your instructions are more valuable to me than millions in gold and silver. You made me; you created me. Now give me the sense to follow your commands. May all who fear you find in me a cause for joy, for I have put my hope in your word. I know, O Lord, that your regulations are fair; you disciplined me because I needed it.

Many have knowledge, but few have wisdom. Many make statements of belief, but few have proven their statements by having a trusting relationship with God. Those who have both, are strengthened against the snares of Satan and equipped for the service of God. We are most apt to wander from God when we are comfortable with this world's goods. Afflictions do a moral service for us. We are constantly dealing with the element of affliction in our spiritual lives. The mission may bring some enlightenment to the darkness in us or reveal the call to duty. The mission of the afflictions may be to master a spirit of self-will preventing one from taking life into their own hands. The mission of pain may be to bring one to a state of humility and self-distrust while exalting one to a place of faith and trust. Pain and suffering can be emotional, mental, physical or spiritual. Hebrews 11 reveals the mission of pain and suffering in these six words: *"their weakness was turned to strength...."* We often focus on the faith of those in that chapter but forget that before their faith, there was pain and suffering that brought them to a turning point. I am a witness to the eye-opening power of pain and suffering. Only by the grace of God can you survive *"The day after that day."* David stated in Psalm 119:67 (NLT2): *"I used to wander off until you disciplined me; but now I closely follow your word."*

The Psalmist speaks here of lessons learned the hard way. There was a time when he was far more likely to go astray from God's Word and the wise life revealed there. Yet, under a season of affliction, he was now devoted to the Word of God. Our trials act as a barbed wire fence to keep us in the Lord's vineyard, but our prosperity is a gap through which we go astray. Poverty brings its pains and temptations, but prosperity also tempts and tries. Wealth often does more "to" a man than it does "for" him, because it can lull the soul to sleep in its comforts. Job was Godly, though wealthy and wealthy though Godly. Humility and prosperity do not always go together, but such is surely possible. Godly men can do without wealth, but wealthy men cannot do without God. Job knew this. Some people can faithfully endure adversity, only to turn away from God in prosperity. Others who stand in prosperity fall in times of adversity. Job withstood the pressures of trials of both.

In this Christian life, we are constantly dealing with the mission of affliction. It may come at any time or on any day. The experience brought about by afflictions, makes plain the practical life of duty and relationship to God. It exposes any self-will that may be growing, which leads the believer to try and take life into his own hands. It also brings the believer into a state of humility and self-distrust, which inclines him to keep well within the limits of God's Word. If you remember a time in which you had no trouble, you also may probably recollect that during that same time, your faithfulness was weak, but temptations were strong. Before your affliction, God was a part time lover, but afterwards, if you responded in the right way, you were purified from your drifting ways by those afflictions and got very close to God.

Affliction does to the believer what cold water does when thrown on a sleeping man. It awakens you. Afflictions get your attention; they compel you to consider the reason for the shocking wake-up call, and they seek answers to the urgency of being awakened so suddenly. When afflictions are so grievous that we can do nothing, we then have a chance to think. If life goes on without tribulations or trials, we can develop a mind of independence. How can a person remain dependent on God, if they are surrounded by prosperity by their seemingly own doing? When affliction comes, it makes one stop, think, then look back to where and how far they have come. They then are able to look up to God that brought them this far.

Spiritual Lessons:

❖ Pain is the fruit of sin, but the grace of God is often made a means of good to the soul. When afflictions have done their work, they will be removed.

❖ Many make statements of belief, but few have proven their statements by having a trusting relationship with God. Those who have both, are strengthened against the snares of Satan, and equipped for the service of God.

❖ The mission of the afflictions may be to master a spirit of self-will preventing one from taking life into their own hands.

❖ If you remember a time in which you had no trouble, you also may probably recollect that during that same time, faithfulness was weak, and temptation was strong.

Chapter 10
The Believer's Ultimate Question

Who do YOU say that I am? Mathew 16:15

O ur beliefs must be aligned with who God says Jesus is if we are to benefit from His promises. There are many perceptions as to who and for what purpose Jesus came. What if Jesus is not who you think He is? The gospel records several critical, heart-searching, and powerful questions that Jesus sincerely asked those around him. Consider Luke 18:8: *"When the Son of Man comes, will he find faith on earth?"* or again, in Luke 6:46: *"Why do you call me 'Lord, Lord' and not do what I tell you?"* From a personal perspective *"Who do you say that I am?"* All are good questions designed to keep us honest. They are serious questions because they demandingly cut to the very core of our relationship with God and Christ. Your attitude should be the same as that of Christ Jesus:

Who, being in the very nature of God, did not consider equality with God something to be grasped, but made himself nothing, taking the very nature of a servant, being made in human likeness. And being found in appearance as a man, he humbled himself and became obedient to death, even death on a cross! Therefore God exalted him to the highest place and gave him the name that is above every name, that at the name of Jesus, every knee should bow, in heaven and on earth and under the earth, and every tongue should confess that Jesus Christ is Lord, to the glory of God the Father. ~Philippians 2:5-11 (NIV)

Being a Christian means believing and confessing that Jesus is the Messiah, but our views of what a Messiah should be doesn't always fit Jesus. Over the many years that I have been a believer in Jesus Christ, I have heard it all on what one has to do to get saved or stay saved. A person is saved when He believes that Jesus is the Lord of Creation and that Jesus saved them from their sins when He died and rose again. It is achieved by believing that God is righteous and merciful and gracious. It is believing that God provided a Savior for all mankind who trusts and believes in Him for their salvation. Believers, by confessing Jesus Christ, are confessing to the actual meaning of the name of the person. God's Salvation to us is not achieved by reciting some words or by the obedience of being baptized in water in the name sent to save them. The name "Jesus Christ" actually means "the anointed Savior of Jehovah." In the gospel of John 1:12, it is written that *God came into the world in the form of a man (Jesus) and the world did not know Him but as many as received Jesus He has given the power to become sons of God.* John said that salvation comes by receiving Jesus. When people say they believe in Jesus, but then they describe attributes that are not those that the Gospel outlines about Jesus, they do not know Christ even if they think they believe in Him. Below are some attributes that is described about Christ in the Word:

- Our Holy, crucified Redeemer, Compassionate loving savior, and Author of our Salvation
- That great shepherd of the sheep

- The shepherd and bishop of our souls, the Father of mercies, the God of comfort.
- The Lion of the Tribe of Judah
- The Author and Finisher of our faith
- The Son of righteousness
- The Branch
- The Mediator of the New Covenant
- The only Mediator between God and man
- The root and offspring of David
- The Good Shepherd

The Old and New Testaments are full of passages that say we are saved by God's grace through our belief in Jesus Christ. The biblical truth is that we are saved by God's grace through our faith by believing and trusting in Jesus. Abraham was saved because he believed God. Noah was saved because he believed God. The thief on the cross was saved by asking the Lord to remember him when Yeshua came into His kingdom showing that He believed that Yeshua was the promised One sent by God. All the apostles were saved by believing that Jesus was the Messiah, the Anointed one, sent from God. The book of Acts is filled with many who were saved by hearing and believing that Jesus was the Christ, the anointed, risen Savior from God. The list is countless. Some say you must also have good works because it is a measure of faith, but I say that scripture teaches that some saved will not have many or any good works. Some believers who were living in flagrant sin during the time of Paul were turned over to the devil for destruction of the flesh so that their souls would be saved in the judgment of Jesus. Consider what is written in 1 Corinthians 3:15: *If any man's work shall be burned, he shall suffer loss: but he himself shall be saved; yet so as my fire.* Also Consider 1 Corinthians 3:5:

To deliver such a one unto Satan for the destruction of the flesh, that the spirit may be saved in the day of the Lord Jesus.

Some will say that this is cheap Christianity, but it is actually free for us and costly for God. Many will quote the passage that says even devils believe and they tremble as "proof text" that it takes more than just belief in Jesus to be saved, but there are scores of passages that tell us that we are saved through our belief in Jesus Christ: *Thou believest that there is one God; thou doest well: the devils also believe, and tremble. (James 2:19)*

It is true that devils also believe that there is "one God" but the passage does not say that devils believe or trust in the Savior God sent for redemption. Scripture reveals that the only thing they trusted the Son of the Most High God for when He was on earth dealing with them was their eventual sentence to the pit! Belief in the Son for salvation is the requirement. The question that's posed to all believers is, "Who do you say that Jesus is?" The answer to that question will be very critical in your time of crisis. With that brief inquiry comes the most challenging and important questions we would ever face. We can spend much time in service and make bold claims about the identity and authority of Christ, but there comes a time when we either believe or deny certain teachings.

Who do you say Jesus is? Your response will determine not only your values and lifestyle, but your eternal destiny as well. I have come to understand that faith is intellectually and experiential. Intellectually, by faith, I accept God's Word as to who He is, what He has done, is doing, and will do. Experientially, my faith has not been tested in certain areas and is unproven. Job is my example of tested and untested faith. Before testing Job, God, through His foreknowledge, had declared him righteous. Knowing that Job's faith would prove to be genuine, God knew that he would persevere. However, Job didn't know himself. There were areas of untested faith in Job's life that caused him to struggle. In the end, Job confessed of the faith that was based on what he had heard as opposed to the faith based on what he had gained through experience. What he had heard was a statement of faith, but what he had experienced was a testimony of faith.

"I had only heard about you before, but now I have seen you with my own eyes. I take back everything I said, and I sit in dust and ashes to show my repentance."
Job 42:5-6

This is the experience that Job attained through his affliction. In the end, it proved to be worth all the agony and misery of his bitter pain and suffering. The last scene of Job is one of joy and beauty, tranquility and triumphant faith. When we look at the close of Job's life, we marvel at the brightness of the morning sun as it rises upon a life which has been refreshed and strengthened. The hero, weary and battle-scared from his bout with the adversary, lives to smile again and to enjoy days of peace and prosperity, friendships and family ties. Truly he emerged from the crucible of trials with riches more precious than gold, a faith tested, tried and proven! He was able to enjoy life on a higher, holier, and happier plane than he had ever known before. Only after the clouds passed over and the purpose of God appears, will we have a testimony of faith. Job contrasted his experiential faith in God with his former intellectual hearsay knowledge. This is what Job possessed in the old days. This is not to say that he was without any religious experience in those prosperous times, but the shallowness of it in comparison to what he had attained made it look of little worth. Most of us begin this way. We hear of God by the hearing of the ear. This is especially true in a Christian country. Here, we seem to breathe a Christian atmosphere and Christian ideas float in upon us unsought, but the faint perception of God that is acquired in this way cannot be of very great value to us. Historical facts can only be known by testimony, and the facts of the gospel must reach us through "the hearing of the ear." But we have not gone very far when we have only come to understand and believe in the historical character of those facts. We are still only among the antiquarian relics at a museum. There is no life in such a knowledge, and it has little influence over us. The effects of experiential faith is that it humbles the person. No longer will you boast of your own strength or think more highly of yourself than you ought to think. Experiential faith awakens and shows you your unworthiness and leads you to praise God for His mercy, for His grace, and for His love. In the light of God's grace, we not only see our smallness, we recognize our Creator as Redeemer and Provider.

More than ever, I have come to understand that we never know ourselves until we see ourselves in the light of God. Much of my belief is based on what I have read and heard about God. This is not to minimize faith in who He is. I also have much testimonial faith. God has performed some great work in my life. Yet I realize that there are some untested areas that I have only heard about. In 2017, when my son Kaneil died, an untested area of my faith awakened some unbelief in me that caused me to search my heart and evaluate what I really believed. It revealed what unbelief was in me. The lesson I learned through it all was that *"You don't really know what you believe until it's time to believe it."* The passing of my son was untested faith that opened my eyes and taught me to never testify of what I can do, but to only testify of what I have gone through and come out on other side of. As Christian believers, we must come to understand that at the heart of the matter is that God will never put more on us than we can bear. If He has allowed us to go through a valley experience, a wilderness experience, or some painful loss, it is because He knows that we will be able to bear it. It is all for the purpose of purification. God will heal you, comfort you, and bring you out on the other side to victory. His Word will accomplish all that God says it will and His promises over your life will not return unto Him void. As for Job, he never knew that he had been the central figure in the giant controversy that involved all the forces of heaven and hell, but he passed his tests and overcame his affliction. The most poignant part of the story is that Job never blamed God, nor did he curse God as he had been told to do. Job's story was not only for Job's benefit alone, but also for our edification and encouragement. My son passing away was a devastating stab to my heart that saddened me to my chore, but I still trust God, love Him, and will continue to serve Him. The truth of the matter is that the Lord gives and the Lord taketh away. Blessed be the name of the Lord!

Spiritual Lessons:

❖ God's Salvation to us is not achieved by reciting some words or by the obedience of being baptized in water in the name sent to save them.

❖ When people say they believe in Jesus, but then they describe attributes that are not those that the Gospel outlines about Jesus, they do not know Christ even if they think they believe in Him.

❖ Who do you say Jesus is? Your response will determine not only your values and lifestyle, but your eternal destiny as well.

❖ The effects of experiential faith is that it humbles the person. No longer will you boast of your own strength or think more highly of yourself than you ought to think.

❖ As Christian believers, we must come to understand that at the heart of the matter is that God will never put more on us than we can bear.

About the Author

Dr. Eric H. Jones, Jr.

Vision, and a heart compelled to do the will of God are the attributes which motivate pastor/leader, Eric H. Jones, Jr. As Founder and Senior Pastor of Koinonia Worship Center & Village, his positive influence and leadership have evolved beyond the walls of the church.

Dr. Jones is a graduate of Attucks high school Class of 1965; Charron Williams Para-medical College; and Southern Baptist Seminary Extension. Pastor Jones is also a Vietnam Veteran. Before entering the ministry, he worked in the area of pharmaceutical quality control as Lab Supervisor and General Manager of blood banks. Because of his humble spirit and many accomplishments, Dr. Jones was bestowed an Honorary Doctorate Degree of Divinity from Saint Thomas Christian University, Jacksonville, FL. in December 2015. Dr. Jones has been a pastor for over 40 years and he continues to serve the Lord and serve as Shepherd of the Sheep that God has given to him.

In 2005, Dr. Jones was elected to serve Broward County Florida's 31st city as the first Mayor of the City of West Park. He served for 16 years total. Dr. Jones is married to Bloneva Jones and they are blessed with three sons: Elder Derrick Jones, Kaniel Jones who preceded them in death, and State Senator Shevrin Jones. They are the proud grandparents of seven grandchildren, six boys and one girl.

CPSIA information can be obtained
at www.ICGtesting.com
Printed in the USA
LVHW081656180122
708821LV00016B/1063